THE *HEALTHY*
BACK
EXERCISE
BOOK

THE *HEALTHY*
BACK
EXERCISE
BOOK

ACHIEVING & MAINTAINING A HEALTHY BACK

Deborah Fielding,
with Simon Fielding, OBE

TED SMART

Dedicated to our daughters Hannah and Charlotte,
who make everything we do worthwhile.

This edition produced for
THE BOOK PEOPLE LTD
Hall Wood Avenue, Haydock,
St Helens, WA11 9UL

Note from the publisher
Every effort has been taken to ensure that all information in this book is correct and
compatible with national standards generally accepted at the time of publication.
This book is not intended to replace consultation with your doctor or other health-
care professional. The authors and publisher disclaim any liability, loss, injury or
damage incurred as a consequence, directly or indirectly, of the use and application
of the contents of this book.

This book was conceived, designed and produced by
THE IVY PRESS
The Old Candlemakers, West Street, Lewes, East Sussex BN7 2NZ

Creative Director: Peter Bridgewater
Design Manager: Tony Seddon
Designer: Alan Osbahr, Andrew Milne
Publisher: Sophie Collins
Editorial Director: Steve Luck
Editor: Sarah Bragginton, Mandy Greenfield
Studio Photography: Mike Hemsley at Walter Gardiner Photography, Zul Mukheida
Illustrations: Michael Courtney, Guy Smith
Picture Researcher: Liz Eddison

Printed in Singapore by Star Standard Industries (Pte) Ltd

CONTENTS

INTRODUCTION

If you are currently suffering from, or have recently recovered from, an episode of back pain, you are not alone! At least 60 per cent of us will suffer from debilitating back pain at some stage in our lives. Back pain can affect anyone, regardless of age, sex or occupation. While most cases are not serious and recover relatively quickly, it can have a major impact on your quality of life. By following the advice and exercises in this book you can help speed your recovery and prevent problems recurring in the future.

right *Learning to carry heavy loads in the correct way will help prevent back problems.*

below *Twisting the body awkwardly can strain the muscles and ligaments of your back.*

One reason why back problems are so common is that in industrialized societies we tend to lead relatively sedentary lives. Many of us sit at desks or in cars for much of the working day and spend an ever-increasing proportion of our leisure time in sedentary activities such as watching television. Lack of physical exercise causes muscles to lose their strength and tone, and joints can easily become stiff, reducing the overall flexibility of our spines. These factors all combine to make the back more susceptible to strain and injury when we undertake even apparently undemanding everyday tasks.

It is recognized that exercise helps low back pain in several ways. First, it strengthens the back muscles and improves flexibility. Second, exercise increases blood flow to the muscles and joints, including those of the spine, so that they are better nourished and healthier. Lastly,

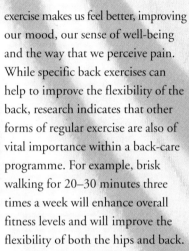

exercise makes us feel better, improving our mood, our sense of well-being and the way that we perceive pain. While specific back exercises can help to improve the flexibility of the back, research indicates that other forms of regular exercise are also of vital importance within a back-care programme. For example, brisk walking for 20–30 minutes three times a week will enhance overall fitness levels and will improve the flexibility of both the hips and back.

Many of you reading this book will probably be suffering from, or have recently suffered, an episode of back pain and are looking for ways to alleviate the pain and, hopefully, to prevent the problem recurring. Many back-care professionals, such as osteopaths, chiropractors and physical therapists, are now stressing the value of self-help measures such as exercise, stretching and correct posture in the speedy resolution and possible prevention of back problems. It is never too early to develop good posture and take adequate, appropriate exercise. Likewise, it is never too late to learn how to correct poor postural habits and increase physical activity for better overall health, well-being and a back that is able to withstand the daily stresses and strains that we place upon it.

By reading this book you will learn simple exercises and other techniques to assist your back. These should not only help to relieve back pain if you are currently suffering, but also help to maintain your back in good condition long after you have recovered. Even if you are one of the lucky ones who have never experienced back pain, by learning and practising regularly the exercises and techniques on the following pages you might avoid becoming yet another back-pain statistic in the future!

left *Self-help measures have a major role to play in alleviating back pain and preventing it recurring.*

HOW TO USE THIS BOOK

Whether you are suffering from back pain, have a tendency to recurrent back problems or simply want to improve the flexibility of your body, this book provides the information you need to achieve a healthier back. While it is not a substitute for expert professional advice and care, the exercises and other techniques that are described can set you on the road to recovery if you are one of the millions of people who suffer from back pain. By following the exercises in this book you will improve the strength and flexibility of your back, allowing you to get more out of life.

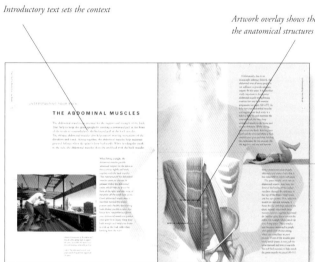

Introductory text sets the context

Artwork overlay shows the relationship of the anatomical structures described

Part One explains how the various structures of the spine – joints, muscles and ligaments – work in combination. It also explores the causes of back pain.

If you are currently experiencing debilitating back pain or are uncertain whether you should begin exercising your back, do seek advice from your doctor or back-care specialist before attempting the self-help measures that are recommended here. Health professionals who specialize in back problems include osteopaths, chiropractors and physical therapists.

The Healthy Back Exercise Book is divided into eight parts. Part One provides an introduction to the bones, muscles and other structures that make up your back and describes some of the most common causes of back pain. The ways in which different types of exercise can benefit your back are explained in detail in Part Two.

Part Three is devoted to helping you determine which exercise will be most suitable for your particular back problem and contains essential warnings about when to seek professional help. It will also tell you how to exercise without strain.

Parts Four to Six contain graduated programmes of exercise designed to help you increase the flexibility and strength of your back through carefully planned stages. The introductory pages in each part explain how to select the exercise you need for your own healthy back programme. In Part Four you are introduced to a series of basic exercises designed for those with an acute back problem and for those starting an exercise programme for the first time. Having mastered these simple exercises, you can then move on to the slightly more challenging programme described in Part Five. Part Six contains instructions for back-maintenance exercises that, if practised regularly, will help to maintain flexibility and the strength of your back.

As well as following an exercise programme, it is also important to consider how you use your back during everyday activities. Part Seven contains simple exercises that can be practised easily in the workplace to help relieve muscle tension and prevent back strains. It also contains helpful advice on posture. Part Eight is devoted to advice for pregnant women, who are especially susceptible to low back pain. In this section there are suggestions for gentle exercises that can help with posture and relieve the additional strain caused by carrying a developing baby.

The final section of the book contains useful reference material, including a glossary of terms, useful addresses, a list of suggested further reading and an index.

Sample programme breaks the exercises into groups and suggests which ones to combine

The opening text summarizes the aims of this part of the book

Introductory spread to the exercise sections explains which exercises to do, how often and in what order.

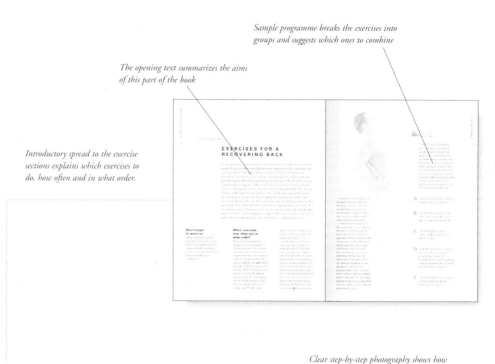

Clear step-by-step photography shows how the body should be positioned

Step text describes exactly how to carry out each action

The main exercise sections (Parts Four to Six) cover every situation from acute back problems to the recovering back and an ongoing maintenance programme.

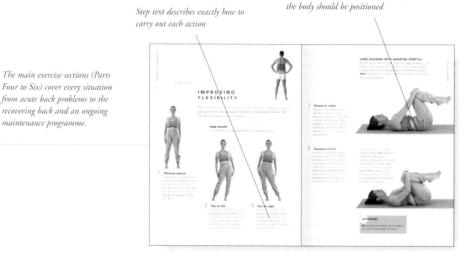

Full-colour photographs amplify points made in the text

Part Seven looks at exercises for the working day, including desk stretches, how to maintain good posture and exercise while travelling.

BEFORE YOU START

Before you start any exercise programme it is important that you know what you want to achieve. Unless you commit yourself to a particular outcome, it is difficult to maintain the motivation to continue. The most important thing to remember is to decide upon your desired outcome and state it in a precise and positive way. It is a strange fact that the unconscious mind cannot recognize negative statements. For example, if you are told, 'Don't think about pink kangaroos', you would probably think about a pink kangaroo before telling yourself not to think about it! While it is understandable that if you are suffering from back pain, you want your back to be pain-free, it is much easier to motivate yourself towards something positive that you want than it is to move away from something that you don't want. So rather than thinking in terms of 'I want my back to stop hurting' or 'I want to lose the pain in my back', turn this into a positive intention, such as 'I want a comfortable, flexible back that I can rely on'.

right *A healthy back will enable you to have more fun with your family.*

below *Be prepared to adapt and revise your exercise programme according to your progress.*

Another important factor in helping to maintain motivation is to look at the positive benefits of achieving and maintaining your desired outcome. For example, having a more flexible and stronger back might encourage or enable you to have more fun playing with your children, or to begin a new pastime or recreation. Once you have decided what your positive outcome should be and the benefits that achieving it will bring you, it is worth writing it down so that you can refer to it in the weeks ahead to remind you of your primary motivation for undertaking the exercise programme.

Setting your goals

Of course it is important to set yourself achievable goals and to start exercising gently. You can then increase your programme over the coming weeks.

● Remember not to try to do too much too soon.

● Begin with the starter exercises in Part Four and plan your exercise routine for the week.

● Be prepared to adapt and revise your programme according to the progress you make and the way your back responds to the exercises. Do not worry if you spend more time than anticipated on any part of the programme – it is not a race. The important thing is that you are maintaining your exercise commitment and are making progress. Mild stiffness or aching is sometimes experienced the day after you have begun new exercises. This is nothing to be worried about and should soon wear off.

● Once you are able to progress from the initial exercises in Part Four, try to build variety into your choice of exercises and general fitness activities. This not only helps to maintain interest, but also helps to exercise different muscle groups and tissues.

● In addition to the specific exercises described in this book, try to increase your level of general physical activity.

WHERE AND WHEN TO EXERCISE

It is worth giving a bit of thought to exactly where and when you will exercise, because establishing the right framework early on will make incorporating an exercise programme into your daily schedule that little bit easier. The clothes that you wear to exercise in and the accessories that may be helpful should also be considered, together with all the essential safety advice.

below *An exercise mat or folded blanket will provide additional cushioning for your back.*

Where to exercise?

Creating a space for exercise should not pose a problem. In the early stages it is helpful if you can be undisturbed, so that you can concentrate on performing the exercises correctly. So choose a quiet place away from the hustle and bustle of family life. All you need is an area big enough to lie down in, with a little space to spare all round. The room should be warm and well ventilated. Plenty of natural light can also help to provide an invigorating atmosphere, but is not essential. An ideal surface is a carpeted floor, and you may like to add an exercise mat or a folded blanket to provide extra cushioning for your back. You might also find it helpful to have a thin pillow or cushion to place under your head and neck for exercises in which you lie on your back. A stable, straight-backed chair is ideal for the seated exercises, although a stool could be used instead.

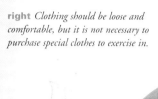

right *Clothing should be loose and comfortable, but it is not necessary to purchase special clothes to exercise in.*

When to exercise?

The time of day you choose to exercise is largely a matter of personal preference and should be chosen to fit in with your daily routine. For some people it is convenient to do their exercises soon after getting up in the morning. For others an evening session is more suitable. It is important, however, that you do not exercise on a full stomach, so try to leave at least a two-hour gap after a main meal. If you are feeling unwell or very tired it may be better to skip or modify your exercise session.

What to wear?

You do not need special exercise clothing. Whenever possible, however, you should wear comfortable, loose-fitting clothing. The exercises themselves can be done barefoot, but you will need suitable shoes, such as trainers, for your warm-up if you plan to go outside or if the floor surface is hard or slippery.

Play it safe

Before you start any of the exercises in this book be sure to read the information on assessing your back problem *(see pages 50–51)* and, if necessary, seek professional advice *(see Useful Addresses, pages 168–169)*. If you have undergone spinal surgery always consult your back-care specialist before undertaking an exercise programme. You should also familiarize yourself with the information on preparation for exercise *(see pages 54–55)* and the general exercise techniques and safety tips *(see pages 56–61)*. Finally, remember to stop any exercise or movement that causes or increases pain or discomfort.

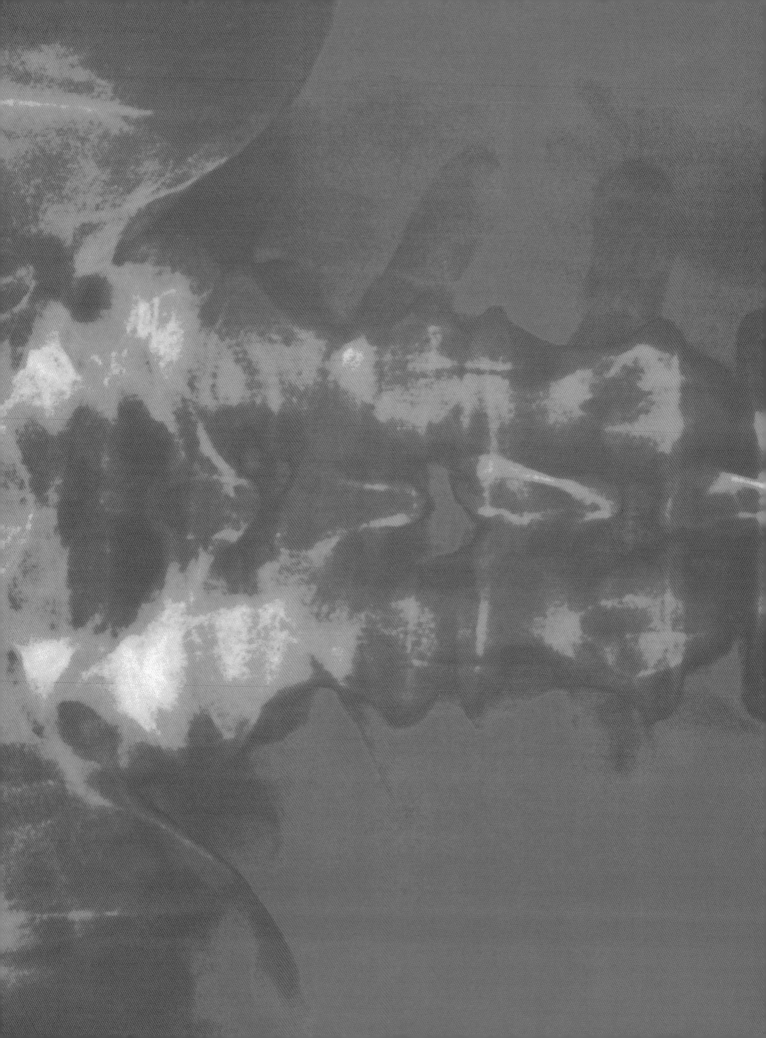

Part One

UNDERSTANDING YOUR BACK

UNDERSTANDING THE SPINE

above *The spine is amazingly flexible and protects the spinal cord.*

The spine is the column of bones, known as vertebrae, that extends from the base of the skull to the pelvis. It supports the head and trunk and enables us to maintain our upright posture. It also provides protection for the main pathway of the nervous system of the body: the spinal cord.

The spine is subdivided into three different regions. The seven vertebrae of the neck are collectively known as the cervical vertebrae, and the skull sits on top of the first cervical vertebra (the atlas). The upper and middle back consists of 12 vertebrae and is known as the thoracic spine, and the lower five vertebrae make up the lumbar spine. Below the lumbar spine and forming part of the pelvis is the sacrum, which is made up of five fused vertebrae. At the end of the sacrum is the small coccyx or tailbone.

Adjacent vertebrae are connected to each other by small joints, the facet joints, which guide movements of the vertebrae and help give stability to the spine. The body of each vertebra is separated from the next by an intervertebral disc. The vertebrae are bound together by two thick ligaments that run the length of the spine and by smaller ligaments that secure one vertebra to another. A number of different muscles also attach to the vertebrae and support and control movements of the spine.

Directly attached to the thoracic spine are the 24 ribs – 12 situated on each side. These are also attached to the sternum (breastbone) at the front of the chest, with the exception of the bottom rib on each side, which is 'floating'. The ribs contribute to the stability of the spine and help to protect the contents of the chest.

Spinal curves

Ideally the spine should be straight when it is viewed from behind. However, vertebrae are linked together in such a way as to produce four natural curves when they are viewed from the side. There are two convex curves, known as the thoracic and sacral curves, which are present at birth, and two concave curves, known as the cervical and lumbar curves, which develop during infancy. These curves are important for giving the back its ability to absorb shocks – for example, when you walk or run.

CERVICAL VERTEBRAE

CERVICAL CURVE

THORACIC VERTEBRAE

THORACIC CURVE

LUMBAR VERTEBRAE

LUMBAR CURVE

SACRUM

SACRAL CURVE

COCCYX

The vertebrae

The vertebrae are not identical; their shape and size differ according to their position in the spine. The largest vertebrae are those of the lumbar region, which have to support the greatest weight.

Each vertebra (except for the atlas, which supports the skull) consists of a solid, almost semicircular front section, which is known as the vertebral body. There is a space (the vertebral canal) in the centre of the vertebra, enclosed by a bony structure called the vertebral arch. It is through this canal that the spinal cord passes.

Three bony projections (or processes) form attachment points for muscles and ligaments (see pages 22–23). These are the two transverse processes and the central, spinous process. It is the spinous processes that can be felt as bony bumps running along the length of your entire spine.

A small hole or channel called the intervertebral foramen lies on each side of the vertebra. These foramina provide both support and protection for the spinal nerves as they emerge from the spinal cord to supply different parts of the body.

FACET JOINT

VERTEBRAL BODY

VERTEBRAL CANAL

SPINOUS PROCESS

TRANSVERSE PROCESS

TRANSVERSE PROCESS

VERTEBRAL BODY

SPINOUS PROCESS

INTERVERTEBRAL FORAMEN

above *Top view of a vertebra.*

right *Side-view of a vertebra.*

left *The four natural curves in the spine show up clearly when the spine is seen from the side.*

INTERVERTEBRAL DISCS AND JOINTS

The individual vertebrae that make up the spinal column are separated by strong, fibrous pads called intervertebral discs. These are situated between the bodies of adjacent vertebrae. The discs can compress to accommodate movement between the vertebrae and thereby allow the spine to bend forwards, backwards and sideways. The important functions of the discs are to act as shock absorbers for the spine and as flexible buffers separating the vertebrae.

Each disc is composed of a fibrous outer covering, called the annulus fibrosus, which encloses a firm, jelly-like substance, known as the nucleus pulposus. When in good health, discs are extremely strong. In fact, if a severe compressive force were applied to the spine, the vertebrae might well fracture before the discs were badly damaged. As we grow older our discs become less flexible and often begin to thin. This process contributes to people losing some height as they get older. Regular and gentle exercise can, however, help to maintain the health and flexibility of your discs, and this is especially important if you spend long periods of your day sitting or driving.

below *An X-ray of a side-view of the cervical spine shows the facet joints between adjacent vertebrae.*

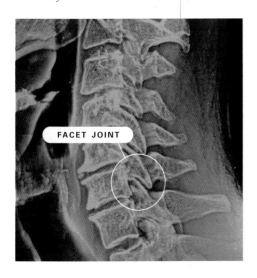

FACET JOINT

Facet joints

These small joints are found in pairs and are situated between the upper and lower surfaces of adjacent vertebrae. The surfaces of the joints are covered with protective cartilage and are enclosed by fibrous, fluid-filled capsules. In a healthy spine the facet joints move smoothly over each other and guide the movements of the vertebrae. Strain of the joints or their surrounding tissues can give rise to protective spasm in the associated spinal muscles. This in turn can compress the facet joints, reducing their mobility and causing local inflammation. Strain of the facet joints is a very common cause of back pain.

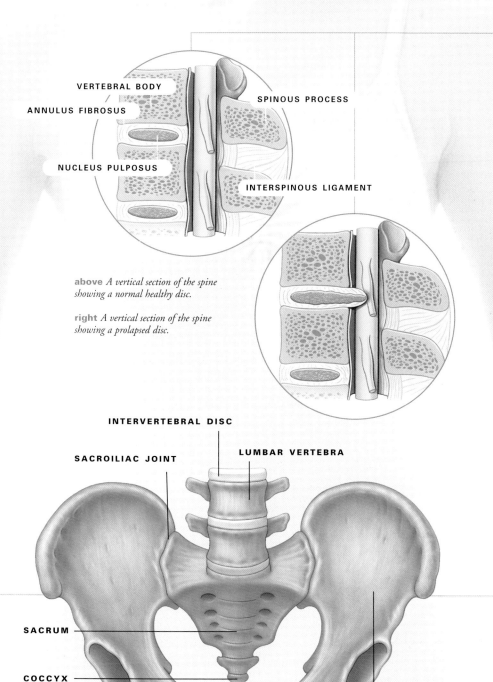

VERTEBRAL BODY

ANNULUS FIBROSUS

SPINOUS PROCESS

NUCLEUS PULPOSUS

INTERSPINOUS LIGAMENT

above *A vertical section of the spine showing a normal healthy disc.*

right *A vertical section of the spine showing a prolapsed disc.*

INTERVERTEBRAL DISC

SACROILIAC JOINT

LUMBAR VERTEBRA

SACRUM

COCCYX

ISCHIUM

INNOMINATE BONE

PUBIC SYMPHYSIS

above *The pelvis consists of a group of immensely strong bones, which are attached to the spine at the lumbar vertebrae and have deep sockets on either side into which the thigh bones fit.*

What is a 'slipped disc'?

Discs actually do not slip, but this is a common term used to describe disc problems. Certain repetitive strains (especially twisting movements when the spine is flexed) can, over time, weaken and damage the annulus of the disc. This can cause the disc to bulge and sometimes the jelly-like nucleus pulposus can herniate into the vertebral canal. This is often referred to as a 'prolapsed disc' *(see page 33)*. While the disc itself is not pain-sensitive, if it bulges or herniates it can press on other surrounding structures – such as the ligaments, nerves or even the spinal cord – and cause considerable pain and disability. If you do have a bulging or herniated disc, then no exercises should be undertaken until you have sought the advice of your doctor or back-care specialist.

The pelvis

The pelvis is a basin-shaped bony structure made up of three bones: the two innominate bones (hip bones) and the sacrum. The innominate bones meet in front at the pubic symphysis and at the back form the two sacroiliac joints with the sacrum. The strong ligaments that bind the sacroiliac joints together allow only a small amount of movement. The joint can, however, become painful if strained or damaged, as a result of an awkward twisting movement or a fall. Pain from the sacroiliac joints is usually felt to one side of the lower back or in the buttocks.

THE SPINAL CORD

The spinal cord is a cylindrical-shaped bundle of nerve tissue approximately the thickness of a finger, which runs from the base of the brain to the upper lumbar region of the spine. It is the main nerve pathway and connects the brain to the peripheral nerves that serve the rest of the body. The spinal cord carries signals from the brain to the muscles to stimulate movement and relays signals conveying pain and other sensory information from the rest of the body back to the brain.

The spinal cord itself consists of a butterfly-shaped bundle of grey matter surrounded by white matter. The grey matter contains nerve fibres that send messages to, and receive them from, the spinal nerves. The nerve fibres in the white matter conduct messages up and down the length of the spinal cord. The spinal cord is surrounded by cerebrospinal fluid and enclosed by a protective membrane known as the dura mater.

The spinal cord runs down the vertebral canal in the centre of the vertebrae, which provides strong but flexible protection for this vital communications channel. The close relationship between the spine and the spinal cord means that any damage to the vertebrae can also affect the spinal cord and/or the spinal nerves associated with it, causing pain or abnormal function of the structures supplied by the damaged area.

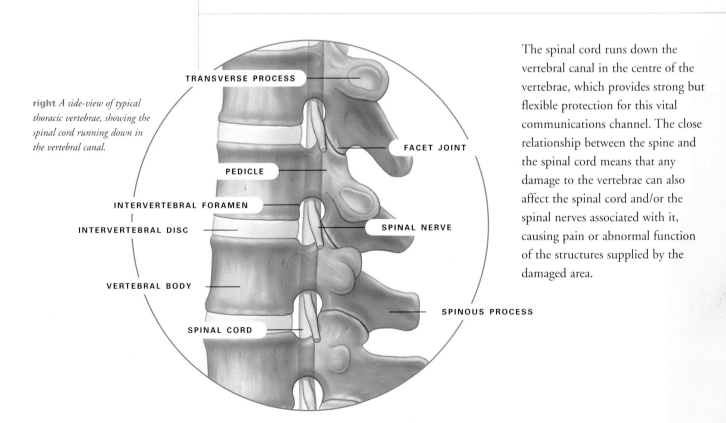

right *A side-view of typical thoracic vertebrae, showing the spinal cord running down in the vertebral canal.*

TRANSVERSE PROCESS

FACET JOINT

PEDICLE

INTERVERTEBRAL FORAMEN

INTERVERTEBRAL DISC

SPINAL NERVE

VERTEBRAL BODY

SPINOUS PROCESS

SPINAL CORD

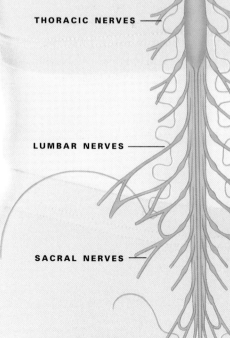

BRAIN

CERVICAL NERVES

DURA MATER

PEDICLE (CUT)

VERTEBRAL BODY

INTERVERTEBRAL DISC

SPINAL CORD

SPINAL NERVE

ENLARGED CROSS-
SECTION OF PART
OF THE SPINAL
COLUMN

THORACIC NERVES

LUMBAR NERVES

SACRAL NERVES

COCCYGEAL NERVES

The spinal nerves

There are 31 pairs of nerves that connect to the spinal cord. These emerge from the spinal cord through the intervertebral foramina between adjacent vertebrae. As the spinal cord only extends about two-thirds of the way down the spinal canal, the lowest nine pairs of nerves run down the vertebral canal before leaving the spine. Each group of spinal nerves serves a separate area of the body, which is usually very localized. This means that pain, numbness or muscle weakness in a particular area can accurately pinpoint the affected spinal nerve.

SPINAL CORD IN VERTEBRAL CANAL

Types of nerve fibre

The spinal nerves contain bundles of nerve fibres of two types: motor fibres that carry signals from the spinal cord to structures such as muscles and glands to control their function, and sensory nerves that carry sensations or pain from the skin, muscles and other structures to the spinal cord. As the spinal nerves exit the spinal cord they branch into two separate roots. One nerve root carries only motor fibres and the other only sensory fibres.

left *Five groups of spinal nerves emerge from the spinal cord and pass information between the brain and various parts of the body.*

BACK MUSCLES AND LIGAMENTS

The mobility, and to some extent the stability, of the back is provided by the complex arrangement of muscles that attach to and act upon the spine, controlling its wide range of movements. Muscles are the tissues that move parts of our body. They consist of bundles of long muscle fibres bound together by connective tissue and are richly supplied with blood vessels and nerves. Muscle fibres respond to nerve stimulation by either contracting to shorten the muscle or relaxing to lengthen it. Most skeletal muscles work in pairs; thus when one muscle contracts, its opposing partner relaxes, allowing movement to take place.

The back muscles are arranged in layers, with the small, deepest muscles extending from one vertebra to the next or its near neighbours, while some of the larger, more superficial muscles run the whole length of the spine and help maintain our upright posture. No muscles cross the midline of the back. The back muscles work with the abdominal muscles (see pages 24–25) to help keep the spine stable and allow it to make its full range of movements without strain.

BICEPS CONTRACTING

TRICEPS RELAXING

BICEPS RELAXING

TRICEPS CONTRACTING

top *Human back muscles relax and abdominal muscles contract to flex the spine.*

above and right *Bending and straightening the arm provides a graphic example of muscles in action. When the biceps muscle at the front of the arm contracts, it shortens in length, pulling up the lower arm, while its opposing muscle, the triceps, relaxes and lengthens. When the triceps contracts, it pulls in the opposite direction, lowering the arm while the biceps relaxes.*

right *Back muscles are arranged in layers. The deepest muscles run from one vertebra to the next, while the more superficial extend the length of the spine.*

Tension, discomfort or pain felt in the muscles of the back is often the result of the spinal muscles contracting more forcibly than normal. This is often referred to as 'muscle spasm' and is usually due to strain or injury to the spinal muscle or other related tissue associated with the spine. If you injure your back, the surrounding muscles can contract forcibly in a painful spasm, which 'splints' the spine in an attempt to prevent the area being moved and possibly damaged further.

Stiffness in muscles can often be the result of unaccustomed exercise. If stiffness is associated with a fitness regime, it can usually be prevented by doing warm-up and cooling-down exercises and stretches. If the stiffness is due to an activity such as gardening, this can sometimes be prevented by doing some stretching exercises before and after the activity.

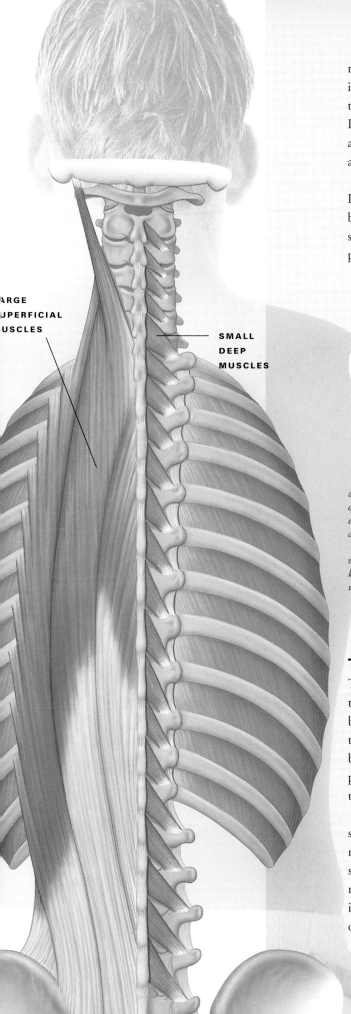

LARGE SUPERFICIAL MUSCLES

SMALL DEEP MUSCLES

CONNECTIVE TISSUE

MUSCLE FIBRES

MYOFIBRILS

MUSCLE FIBRE

above *Muscles consist of bundles of cells called muscle fibres, which are enclosed within an envelope of connective tissue.*

right *Bundles of small strands known as myofibrils are contained within each muscle fibre.*

The ligaments

The ligaments of the spine are made of strong fibrous tissue. These, together with the action of the muscles, serve to make the spine a stable but flexible structure. Two longitudinal ligaments extend vertically along the length of the spine, attaching to the front and back of the vertebral bodies. Shorter intertransverse and interspinous ligaments join the processes of adjacent vertebrae together. Ligaments also attach the base of the spine to the pelvis, and the ribs to the sides of the thoracic vertebrae.

Healthy ligaments are strong and slightly elastic. Those that are subjected to constant strain, through habitual poor posture for example, may become overstretched and lose some of their effectiveness in stabilizing the spine. Ligaments that are overstretched or injured can give rise to pain. This is particularly noticeable in areas such as the neck after it has been subjected to trauma, such as whiplash injury. The ligaments of the sacroiliac joint can also be subjected to strain and can cause pain.

THE ABDOMINAL MUSCLES

The abdominal muscles are essential for the support and strength of the back. They help to keep the spine upright by exerting a downward pull at the front of the trunk to counterbalance the backward pull of the back muscles. The oblique abdominal muscles also help control twisting movements of the shoulders and trunk. Acting together, the abdominal muscles help maintain postural balance when the spine is bent backwards. When bending the trunk to the side, the abdominal muscles share the workload with the back muscles.

When lifting a weight, the abdominal muscles provide additional support for the spine as they contract tightly and work together with the back muscles. This contraction of the abdominal muscles causes an increase in pressure within the abdominal cavity, which helps to brace the front of the spine and take some of the strain off the small facet joints. Good abdominal muscle tone is therefore essential for correct posture and a healthy functioning back. Before you lift or move any heavy item, remember to tighten your abdominal muscles to protect your spine from injury. Keep your back straight and bend your knees to pick up the load, rather than bending from the waist.

above *Contraction of the abdominal muscles while lifting helps to support the spine, even when the back is in a forward-bending, vulnerable position.*

right *The abdominal muscles and psoas muscles help provide support for the spine.*

Unfortunately, due to an increasingly sedentary lifestyle, the abdominal tone of many people is not sufficient to provide adequate support for the spine. It is therefore vitally important to incorporate abdominal-muscle strengthening exercises into any back-exercise programme *(see pages 122–127)*. To help tone your abdominal muscles and support your back make it a habit to draw in, and maintain the contraction of, the very deep abdominal muscle in the lower part of your abdomen. While sitting, concentrate on slowly drawing your navel and the area just below it back towards your spine and then holding the contraction for ten seconds. Do this regularly and you will benefit

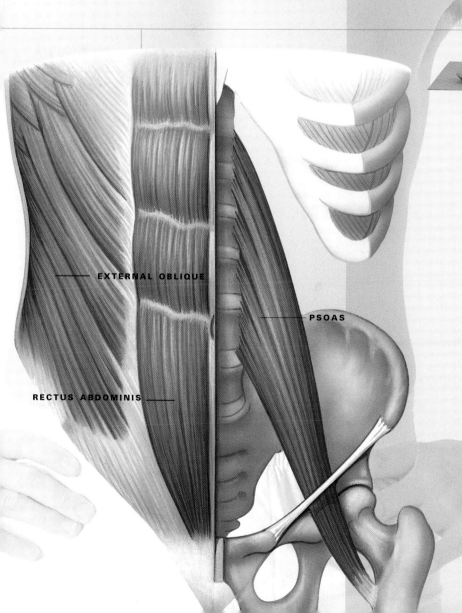

from a toned and more shapely abdomen and a lower back that is less vulnerable to injury and strain.

The psoas muscle, while not an abdominal muscle, runs from the front of the bodies of the lumbar vertebrae through the abdomen to the top of the femur (thigh bone) and has two actions. First, when the muscle on one side contracts, it flexes the hip and thigh towards the chest; second, when both psoas muscles contract together they bend the lumbar spine down towards the pelvis, for example when you sit up from lying down. These muscles may become contracted in people who spend a lot of time sitting, which can contribute to poor posture. If one of the muscles goes into painful spasm, it may pull the spine forward and over to one side. You will find exercises to help stretch the psoas muscle on pages 110–111.

EXTERNAL OBLIQUE

PSOAS

RECTUS ABDOMINIS

MOVEMENT AND FLEXIBILITY

The spine is not a rigid structure and allows a considerable range of movement. The active range of movement in the spine consists of flexion (forward bending), extension (backward bending), lateral flexion (side bending) and rotation (turning) to either side.

All these different movements are achieved by synchronized action of the back and the abdominal muscles *(see page 24).*

above *Bending the head to one side requires lateral flexion of the cervical spine.*

below *The lumbar and thoracic spine rotates to allow the body to twist.*

The full range of possible movement in the back requires that all tissues in the area are healthy and flexible. The bodies of the vertebrae and their discs support most of the weight of the trunk and other compressive forces that pass through them. The discs have to be strong and flexible to allow for movements between each vertebra without tearing, bulging or pressing on surrounding tissues. The surfaces of the facet joints need to glide smoothly over each other, guiding the movements of the spine, and the ligaments need to be strong so that they can prevent any of these movements from going too far. The muscles too have to be in balance, as some have to contract to initiate movement, while others have to relax and lengthen to allow the movement to take place. When bending, postural muscles have to work hard to keep the whole body in balance so that we don't fall over! Even standing involves the coordinated effort of many of

Improving flexibility

Even if your spine and back have become stiff over the years, it is never too late to take steps to improve the situation. Flexibility can be regained, and maintained by regularly performing exercises that gently and progressively stretch stiffened joints, tight muscles and underused ligaments. The exercises in this book will show you how!

the postural muscles, all finely controlled by the nervous system.

The overall mobility and flexibility of the structures of the back can be limited by the effect of injury or lack of use. A reduction of flexibility in one part of the spine may impair its ability to absorb shocks and fulfil its normal range of movement; this can place additional strain on other areas of the spine.

Babies and young children are naturally flexible and generally have a much greater range of movement in their spines than most adults. Flexibility tends to reduce with age due to discs becoming thinner and other tissues becoming less elastic. Muscles can become chronically shortened due to poor posture and the smooth surface of the facet joints can become worn and roughened. It is, however, possible to maintain – or even regain – a good degree of flexibility in the spine throughout all stages of adult life. The muscles, ligaments, discs and joints of your spine are all designed for movement. Therefore spines that are regularly stretched and exercised will become, and remain, more flexible and healthy.

WHO IS AT RISK?

Back pain is one of the most common health problems and almost all of us will suffer from back trouble at some point in our lives. The back is designed for, and thrives on, movement and, provided it is not subjected to abnormal stresses, it becomes stronger and fitter the more it is used. On the other hand, inactivity causes muscles to weaken and joints to become stiff. Our increasingly sedentary lifestyle is undoubtedly one of the major causes of the rising number of back problems. Fortunately, by being aware of the risk factors almost everyone can take steps to reduce the chances of developing back trouble.

above *Carrying a heavy load in one hand places unnecessary strain on the spine.*

top *Squash is a game best suited to younger players because of the risk of rotational injuries.*

Risk factors

Apart from the cumulative effects of a sedentary lifestyle, there are a number of other factors that predispose us to back problems. Younger people are more likely to suffer episodes of acute back pain because they (generally) have a more active lifestyle.

As we grow older, degenerative changes of the spine and discs occur that can predispose us to back pain. Because of this, and because of a general decline in our physical fitness, it is important that, during middle age, certain lifestyle changes are made so that the back is put under less strain.

Middle age is therefore the time to change from high-impact sports such as squash to other, less vigorous sports such as badminton, which do not carry such a risk of causing rotational injury to the spine and other joints, especially the knees. This is also the time to be even more careful when lifting and to ensure that frequent breaks are taken when undertaking any physical activity such as gardening.

Certain occupations – for example manual work – will, by nature of the physical demands that are placed on the back, carry an increased risk of injury.

Pregnant women are also more at risk of back pain. In the later stages of pregnancy certain postural changes occur that place the spine under increased strain. This subject is discussed in detail on pages 158–159.

Anyone who is significantly overweight *(see opposite for how to calculate this)* is also more likely to suffer from back problems. By losing any excess weight you will certainly reduce your risk of suffering from back pain.

Do you need to lose weight?

Being overweight is increasingly a problem for a large proportion of the population, young and old alike. In the US at least 34 per cent of the adult population is overweight. Carrying excess weight puts tremendous additional strain on all weight-bearing joints, especially those of the vertebrae, hips and knees, predisposing you to the development of early osteoarthritis in these areas *(see page 36)*. In particular, excessive weight gain places additional stress on the facet joints of the lower back. This is due to backward-bending, compensatory postural changes that are necessary to balance an enlarged abdomen, similar to the postural changes that take place in later pregnancy. As well as being an additional burden on the musculoskeletal system, being overweight also increases the risk of developing heart disease, high blood pressure, diabetes, gallstones and digestive problems.

In order to decide whether you are overweight – and, if so, by how much – you can calculate your body mass index (BMI). This calculates your weight in relation to your height and gives an estimate of how much of your total weight is made up of fat. When you have calculated your BMI you can then compare it with the standard ranges.

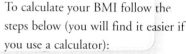

To calculate your BMI follow the steps below (you will find it easier if you use a calculator):

1 Write down your weight in kilograms and your height in metres. For example, 80kg and 1.75m.
2 Divide your weight by your height; e.g. $80 \div 1.75 = 45.7$.
3 Again divide the figure you arrive at by your height; e.g. $45.7 \div 1.75 = 26.1$. In this example your BMI is 26.1.

Now compare your BMI with the following ranges and you will get an indication of whether you are within a healthy weight range.

below 19	*underweight*
19–24.9	*healthy weight*
25–29.9	*overweight*
30–39.9	*obese*
40 and over	*severely obese*

In the example used above a BMI of 26.1 falls in the overweight range. It would therefore be advisable to embark on a programme of healthy eating and increased exercise to bring your BMI into the healthy weight range, by losing at least 5kg.

above *Fast food may be a factor in excessive weight gain and should be eaten in moderation.*

below *A healthy diet that contains a good balance of fresh fruit and vegetables, slow-release carbohydrates and fibre will help to regulate your weight.*

WHAT IS BACK PAIN?

Back pain, like other forms of pain that we experience, is the result of the brain receiving messages from the nerves in a part of the body that is either under strain or has been injured or damaged. These messages are transmitted in the form of chemical and electrical signals from nerve receptors at the site of the pain along the peripheral nerves to the spinal cord, which then relays the pain signal to the brain. All of this takes only a fraction of a second.

above *Severe back pain can be debilitating at any age.*

below right *Pain that is felt in the buttock may be referred pain caused by a prolapsed disc pressing on one of the spinal nerves that form the sciatic nerve.*

below left *When a disc prolapses, the nucleus pulposus can protrude through the annulus fibrosus and press on a spinal nerve.*

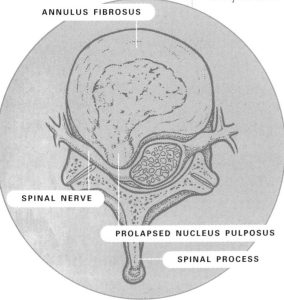

ANNULUS FIBROSUS

SPINAL NERVE

PROLAPSED NUCLEUS PULPOSUS

SPINAL PROCESS

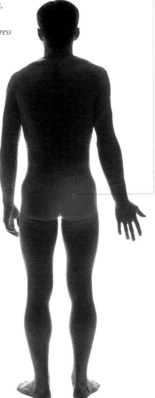

Referred pain

Some underlying back problems can manifest themselves as pain in areas other than the back itself. Known as referred pain, this occurs because of the close relationship of the spine to all the main nerves in the body. For instance, if inflammation, or possibly pressure from a damaged disc, irritates a spinal nerve near its junction with the spinal cord, the resultant pain may be experienced coming from the area served by that nerve. For example, 'sciatica' (pain that can be felt in the buttock or down the back of the leg) is often caused by pressure from a damaged intervertebral disc pressing on one of the spinal nerves that make up the sciatic nerve as it emerges from the spine. Likewise, arm pain may be the result of a similar problem in the lower neck. In severe cases the pain may be accompanied by numbness or muscle weakness in the affected part.

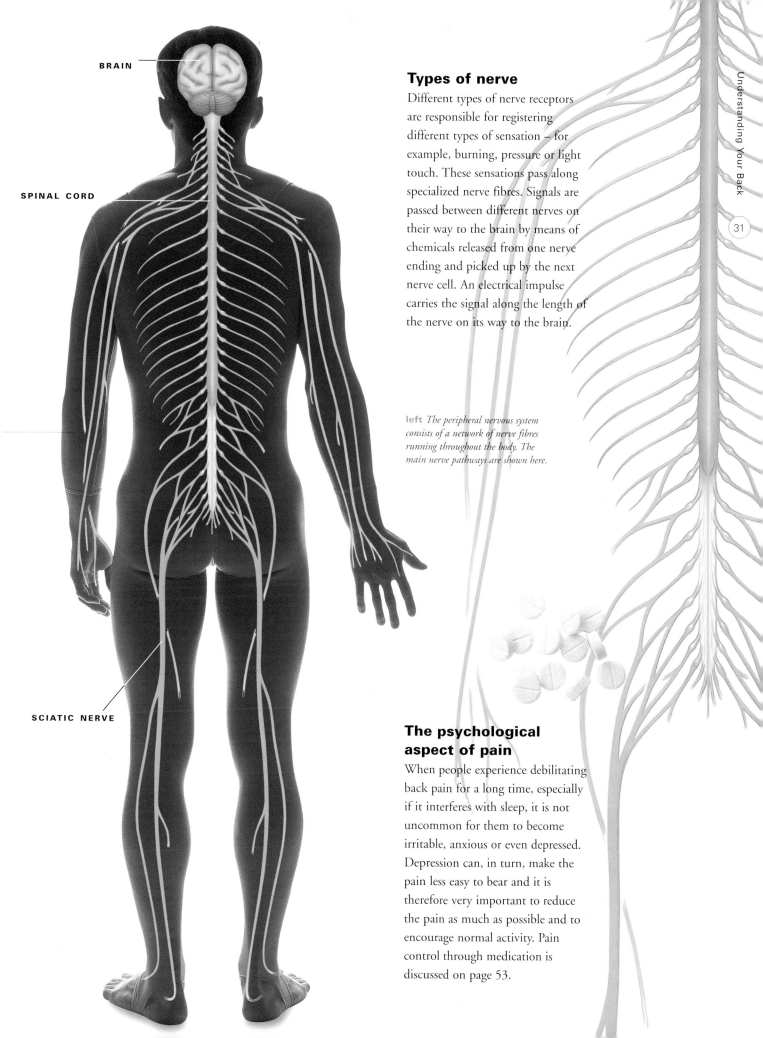

BRAIN

SPINAL CORD

SCIATIC NERVE

Types of nerve

Different types of nerve receptors are responsible for registering different types of sensation – for example, burning, pressure or light touch. These sensations pass along specialized nerve fibres. Signals are passed between different nerves on their way to the brain by means of chemicals released from one nerve ending and picked up by the next nerve cell. An electrical impulse carries the signal along the length of the nerve on its way to the brain.

left The peripheral nervous system consists of a network of nerve fibres running throughout the body. The main nerve pathways are shown here.

The psychological aspect of pain

When people experience debilitating back pain for a long time, especially if it interferes with sleep, it is not uncommon for them to become irritable, anxious or even depressed. Depression can, in turn, make the pain less easy to bear and it is therefore very important to reduce the pain as much as possible and to encourage normal activity. Pain control through medication is discussed on page 53.

ACUTE BACK PROBLEMS

Back pain is often categorized into two main types: acute and chronic. Although relative terms, acute is often used to describe a condition that comes on suddenly and lasts a comparatively short time (up to four to six weeks). It is not necessarily more severe than a long-term, or chronic, problem *(see page 34)*, but often requires immediate treatment. Acute and chronic problems are not totally distinct, in that the former often arise as a result of weaknesses caused by an underlying chronic condition or weakness of the supporting structures of the spine. If unresolved, an acute problem may progress to become a chronic one. Research shows that maintaining the mobility of the back with exercise and an early return to normal activities is the best way to prevent this.

above *The lower back is a common site of acute back pain.*

below *Bending the back while lifting can cause an acutely painful strain injury of the lower spine.*

right *When the back is under strain for any reason, the facet joints may be taken beyond their normal range of movement, causing pain.*

Strain injuries

Most common acute back problems are caused by an injury or a strain. This can occur when a facet joint is taken beyond its normal range of movement. Such strains may be the result of lifting incorrectly (for example, in a twisted position), a fall or an awkward movement – for instance, while playing sport.

Whiplash injuries, which can affect the neck and back, may result from car accidents. In a de-acceleration accident the force of the impact causes the person first to be flung forwards and then backwards. This causes complex strain injuries to the supporting structures of the spine, especially the neck, which may remain painful for months.

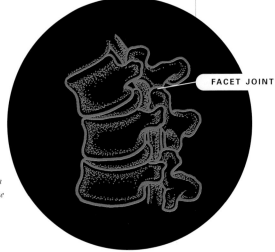

FACET JOINT

right *The structure of the spine is such that it is vulnerable to a range of injuries and weaknesses.*

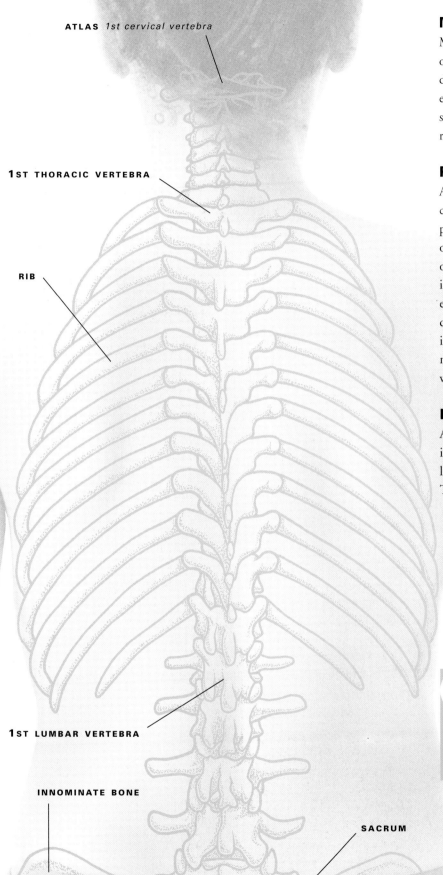

ATLAS *1st cervical vertebra*

1ST THORACIC VERTEBRA

RIB

1ST LUMBAR VERTEBRA

INNOMINATE BONE

SACRUM

Muscle spasm

Muscle spasm *(see page 23)* is a common cause of acute back and neck pain. Spasm may develop the day following a trauma or strain, for example after twisting awkwardly in a game of squash; after heavy lifting; or even after a minor road-traffic accident.

Fractures

A fracture of the vertebrae is another – though comparatively rare – possible cause of acute back pain. It can occur as the result of a serious fall or other trauma. Because of the risk that a fracture of the spine may damage the spinal cord, injuries in which a fracture is suspected require emergency medical treatment. In such cases, do not move the injured person, but seek immediate medical assistance. Fractures are more common in those whose bones have been weakened by osteoporosis *(see pages 36–37)*.

Prolapsed disc

An intervertebral disc may cause acute back pain if it bulges or herniates, pressing on nearby ligaments and/or spinal nerves *(see page 19)*. This is known as a prolapsed disc.

CAUTION

ACUTE BACK PAIN MAY ALSO BE CAUSED BY CERTAIN OTHER MEDICAL CONDITIONS. BE SURE TO GET AN EXPERT DIAGNOSIS. SEE ALSO PAGES 50–53.

CHRONIC BACK PROBLEMS

The term chronic is often used to describe a persistent health problem – in this case back pain – that has been present for a long time, usually for at least several months. Some chronic back pain may be the result of an old injury or trauma, but it commonly arises from habitual misuse of the back. This can be due to poor posture, being overweight or repeatedly carrying out actions that strain the back. In older people chronic back pain may be the consequence of degenerative changes associated with ageing, for example osteoarthritis (wear and tear of the joints, *see page 36*) and osteoporosis (thinning of the bones, *see pages 36–37*). Acquired or developmental abnormalities of the spinal curves, such as kyphosis and scoliosis, can also give rise to chronic back pain.

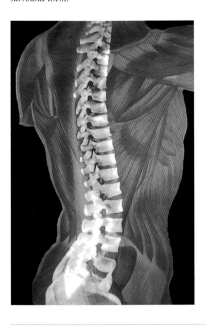

below *A CT scan of a healthy human spine superimposed on a torso shows the relationship of the vertebrae and spinal column to the muscles that surround them.*

Postural stresses

Good posture helps to ensure that the spine is in the best possible position to withstand the stresses and strains that everyday tasks demand of it. Habitual poor posture, however, places additional strain on the spine and its supporting structures, and requires considerable effort to correct it. Very young children usually have excellent posture, but their natural poise is soon lost as they have to adapt to furniture – both at home and at school – that is not made for their size and needs. Most school furniture is designed for a wide age range, the chairs being generally unsupportive of the back. Desks are often at the wrong height and flat, rather than sloped, so that children are forced to slump forward when writing. At home the family computer desk and chair are usually at a height that suits adult members of the family and not the child, so that the child has to assume a strained posture when using the keyboard.

By the time children are teenagers they will probably be carrying excessively heavy school bags between home and school, often slung over one shoulder so that the spine is strained, not just by the heavy load, but also by being pulled to one side. While at school the majority of the day will be spent slumped at a school desk and, once home from school, many more hours will usually be spent in front of the television or computer.

This sedentary lifestyle will, all too often, continue into adult life, with long periods spent sitting at a

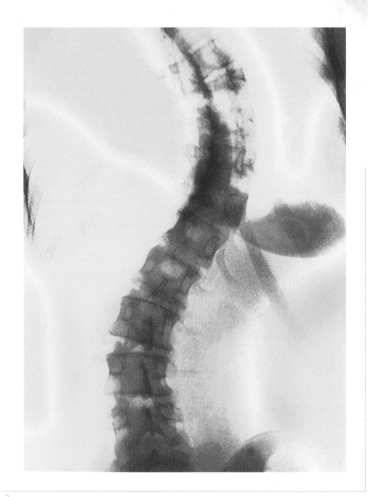

left *The lateral curvature of the thoracic and lumbar vertebrae, as seen on X-ray, is characteristic of scoliosis.*

desk, driving or relaxing on a sofa. Sadly, many recreational activities are becoming increasingly sedentary, with the growth in the home leisure industry. This inactivity results in loss of muscle tone in the abdominal and back muscles, so that the spine is poorly supported and the back is more prone to strain when physical demands are placed upon it. Furthermore, while sitting, the discs of the lumbar spine are subjected to more compressive forces than they are when standing or walking and the supporting ligaments of the spine are placed under greater strain.

The combined effects of habitual poor posture and a sedentary lifestyle can, therefore, be a significant factor in the development of chronic back pain. To help guard against this you can follow the advice on how to sit correctly while you are driving and at the office *(see pages 142–143 and 150–151)*. Guidance on how to improve your posture can also be found on pages 98–99. Additionally, by increasing your overall levels of physical activity and by carrying out the stretching and strengthening exercises described in this book, you will be less likely to suffer back pain that is caused by postural stress.

Kyphosis

This is a term used to describe an exaggerated forward bending of the spine, arising in the upper and mid-thoracic area. It can be caused by a variety of disorders of the bones, including osteoporosis, infections or congenital disorders, and by habitual poor posture.

Scoliosis

This is a deformity in which the spine is bent to one side and is most common in the thoracic and lumbar regions. If one part of the spine bends to one side, then other areas of the spine try to compensate and bend in the opposite direction. This can result in an S-shaped spinal curve when seen from the back. A scoliosis of the spine sometimes develops in childhood, the cause of which is unknown. Other cases are the result of congenital abnormalities of the vertebrae or tilting of the pelvis due to one leg being shorter than the other. A temporary scoliosis can result from an injury to the spine, such as a prolapsed disc. This is often accompanied by back pain and sciatica and will resolve when the injury heals.

Osteoarthritis

Commonly referred to as 'wear and tear' of the joints, osteoarthritis is one of the most common problems associated with ageing and can affect the majority of the joints of the body. Almost everyone over the age of 45 will begin to develop slight signs of osteoarthritic change in some of their joints, especially the weight-bearing ones such as the hips, knees and facet joints of the spine. However, these early changes do not usually give rise to discomfort and may never become a cause of pain.

Osteoarthritis occurs when the protective cartilage covering the joint surface begins to wear. Over the years this can cause a roughening of the joint surface and inflammation in the surrounding tissues. Small bony projections called osteophytes may also develop around the margins of the joint. These can give rise to pain and reduce mobility in the affected joint. Osteoarthritis that affects the facet joints of the lumbar spine will often cause considerable stiffness in the lower back, especially on rising in the morning.

The best way of delaying the development of osteoarthritis in the weight-bearing joints, especially of the lumbar spine, is to keep your weight to a minimum and take plenty of regular, gentle physical exercise. Even if you already have symptoms associated with osteoarthritis, lose weight (if you are overweight) and take regular, appropriate exercise to increase flexibility and tone the muscles that support the affected joints. This will almost certainly give you an improvement in your symptoms and an overall feeling of well-being.

Osteoporosis

Bones are made up of several different layers. The surface of the bone is covered by a thin membrane called the periosteum, which contains blood vessels and nerves. Under this is a hard, dense shell of bone called the compact layer, inside which lies a layer of less dense spongy or cancellous bone. Bundles of a protein called collagen form a framework within the bone and this is covered with various minerals, primarily calcium salts.

This structure gives bone its qualities of resilience, hardness and strength. The calcium salts are constantly being laid down and reabsorbed, this process being controlled by various hormones, including the growth hormone,

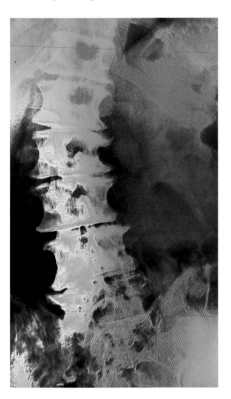

below *Degenerative changes due to osteoarthritis include roughening of the joint surfaces and bony projections around the joint margins.*

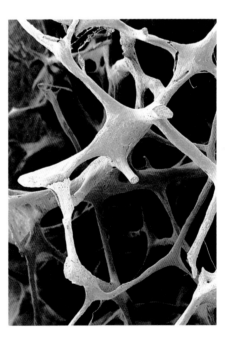

above *Osteoporotic bone – shown here on an electron micrograph – is far less dense than normal bone.*

oestrogen and testosterone. The rate of bone mineralization is rapid during childhood and young adulthood, but levels out during the mid-twenties, and by the age of 35 bone density starts to be lost as part of the normal ageing process, with calcium salts being reabsorbed more quickly than they are replaced. This results in the bone becoming less dense.

Both men and women lose 0.3–0.5 per cent of their bone mass or density each year after their mid-thirties. The term osteoporosis is used to describe the condition in which bones have lost a significant amount of their density, thus losing a degree of strength and becoming more brittle and prone to fracture. The most common sites of fracture for bones that are affected by osteoporosis are the hips, the wrists and the vertebrae.

A significant reduction in bone density occurs in women who no longer produce oestrogen, due (usually) to the menopause or the surgical removal of their ovaries. For this reason osteoporosis is more common in women, affecting one in three women over the age of 50. It does, however, also affect men, one in eight of whom over the age of 50 will develop osteoporosis. Other causes include some hormonal disorders and the prolonged use of corticosteroid medication.

Each year doctors in the UK treat more than 60,000 hip and 40,000 spinal fractures that have been directly caused by osteoporosis, while in the USA 1.3 million fractures are attributed to osteoporosis each year and it is estimated to cost the US economy a staggering $10 billion annually.

When osteoporosis affects the vertebrae, particularly those of the

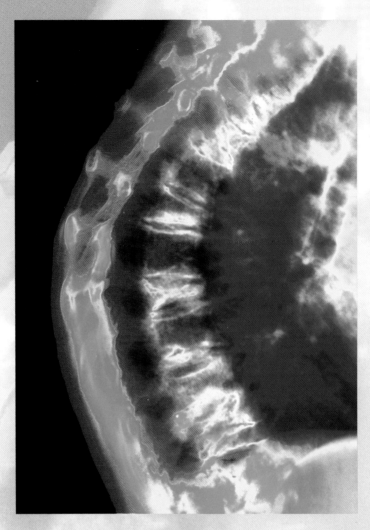

thoracic spine, the front part of the vertebral bodies can become compressed and wedge-shaped, causing a notable increase in the thoracic curve. This distortion can be extremely disabling and may give rise to persistent backache. The bodies of vertebrae that have been affected by severe osteoporosis may also fracture and collapse, causing severe pain.

Measures to help prevent osteoporosis include a well-balanced diet rich in calcium and vitamin D and plenty of weight-bearing exercise. Hormone replacement therapy can reduce the rate at which bone is lost and there are now drugs that encourage the mineralization of bone for people suffering from, or at risk of, osteoporosis.

above *A computer-enhanced X-ray of osteoporosis in the thoracic spine reveals 'wedging' in the front of the vertebral bodies and an exaggeration of the thoracic curve.*

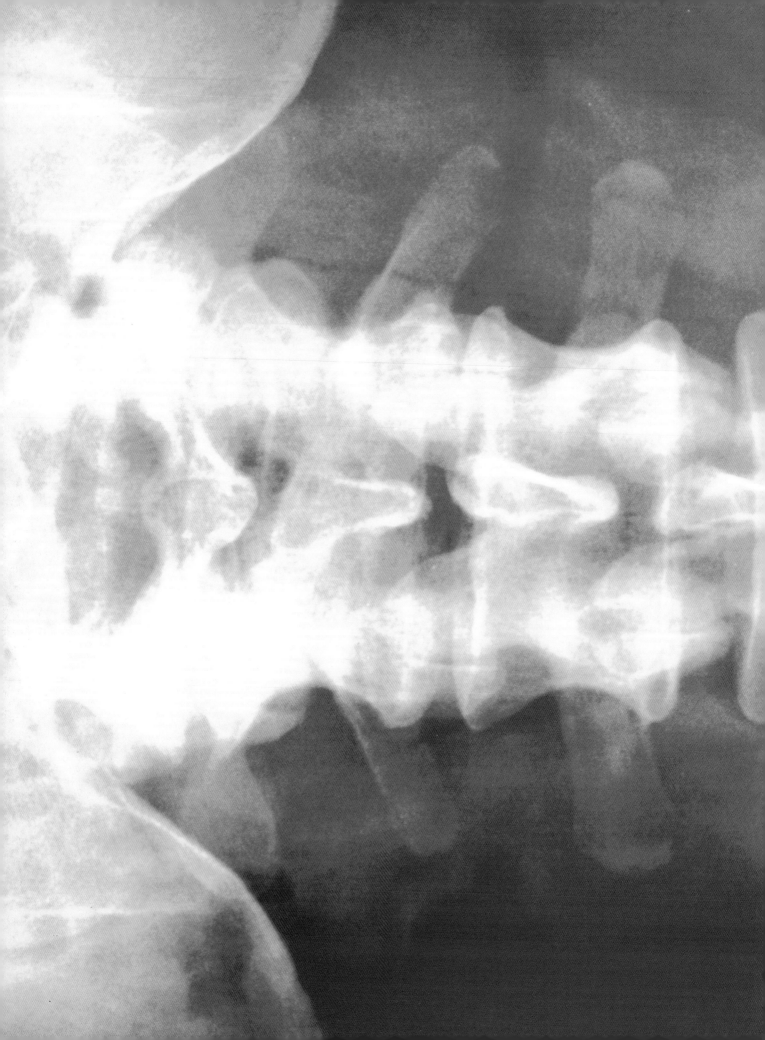

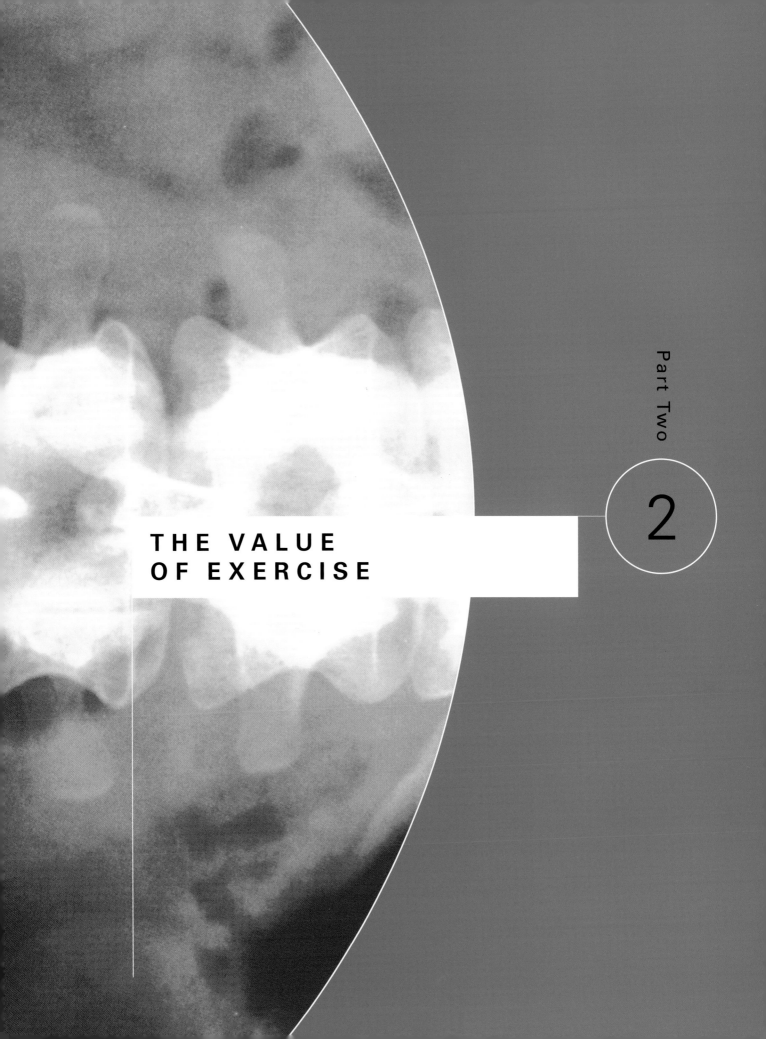

2

THE VALUE
OF EXERCISE

THE VALUE OF EXERCISE

WHY EXERCISE?

Physical exercise is beneficial to health in many ways and can improve the quality of your life, delaying any deterioration in fitness and flexibility due to increasing age and inactivity. Exercise has also been shown to enhance your overall feeling of well-being, providing important psychological benefits.

above *Cycling is good cardiovascular exercise and can help to develop physical stamina.*

Another benefit of exercise is that an improvement in memory function has been reported among older people who embark on a programme of exercise.

Regular exercise can also improve and maintain mobility of the joints by encouraging their full range of movement and by stretching the surrounding tissues. Muscles, too, will benefit from both general and specific exercise, increasing their strength and overall tone. In the case of the back and abdominal muscles, this will help to support and stabilize the spine. This is particularly important, as it helps to protect the back from strain or injury when you are lifting or carrying out everyday activities, such as bedmaking and gardening. Developing the muscles that help maintain good posture *(see page 98)* is the key to changing the way that you use your body.

Excess muscle tension, which may result from emotional stress or habitual poor posture, can also be alleviated by gentle exercise that

makes use of, but does not strain, the muscles. Weight-bearing exercise is especially important, as it helps to maintain bone density and can slow the onset of osteoporosis *(see pages 36–37)*. Even those who have already developed the condition can, to some degree, slow its progression by undertaking suitable regular exercise. Remember that osteoporosis affects men as well as women. To maintain a healthy back, a combination of specific stretching and strengthening exercises with appropriate general exercise, such as regular walking, is ideal. A brisk walk of 20–30 minutes three times a week, which increases your heart and breathing rate, can have a very beneficial effect on overall health.

Regular exercise improves heart and lung function and stimulates the circulation, bringing benefits to every part of the body. This increased circulation also promotes healthy joints, tissues and intervertebral discs, which all benefit from the increased flow of oxygen and essential nutrients carried by the blood.

As well as being good for both mind and body, exercise has also been shown to alter our perception of pain, making it easier to cope with the aches and pains that are often a part of everyday living.

right *Walking is an ideal form of exercise, and is something that the whole family can enjoy.*

above *Swimming is good for those with bad backs, although crawl or backstroke is often better than breaststroke, which may aggravate painful back and neck muscles.*

WHY WARM UP?

Warm-up exercises are the first elements in any exercise routine. They are designed to stimulate the circulation, which increases the supply of oxygen and nutrients to the muscles, preparing them for the more demanding activities that may be required later. Muscles, tendons, ligaments and joints that have been 'warmed up' are more supple and less likely to be strained. An effective warm-up routine also helps to prevent stiffness after exercise provided some cooling-down stretches are performed at the end of the exercise session.

What are warm-up exercises?

Warm-ups fall into two groups: general cardiovascular exercise and gentle stretching exercises to prepare the principal muscle groups of the body for action. Ideally you need to incorporate both types of warm-ups into your exercise programme. However, if you are unable (either physically or due to time constraints) to do the cardiovascular booster, do not omit the gentle stretching exercises *(see pages 80–81)* before you progress to the more demanding stretching and strengthening exercises.

Cardiovascular exercises are, in simple terms, exercises that provide enough physical exertion to speed up your heart rate and increase the depth and rate of your breathing. Exercises that perform this function include running and jogging, cycling, swimming, stepping and brisk walking. For people using this book who are subject to back problems, a short period of gentle

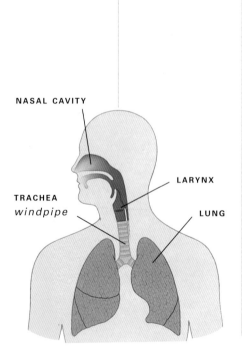

NASAL CAVITY

LARYNX

TRACHEA
windpipe

LUNG

above *Effective exercise should increase the rate of respiration, boosting oxygen levels in the blood.*

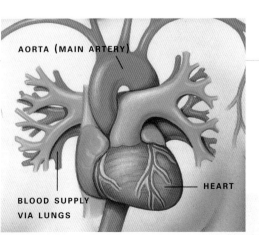

AORTA (MAIN ARTERY)

HEART

BLOOD SUPPLY
VIA LUNGS

left *Exercise increases the body's heart rate and the supply of oxygenated blood to the body.*

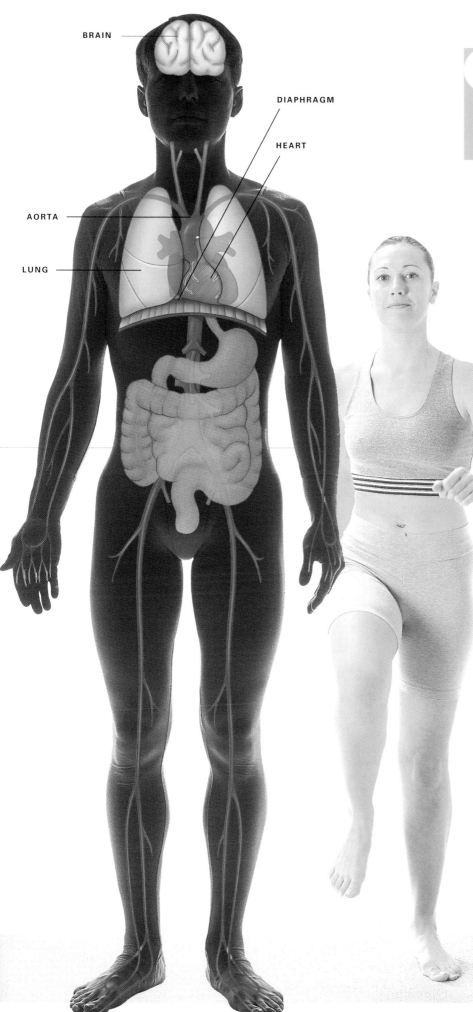

BRAIN

DIAPHRAGM

HEART

AORTA

LUNG

CAUTION

ALWAYS STOP ANY EXERCISE IF YOU
EXPERIENCE CHEST PAIN, FAINTNESS OR
EXCESSIVE SHORTNESS OF BREATH.

cardiovascular exercise is all that is necessary, as more strenuous exercise may risk strain or injury as a result of jarring.

Stretching exercises work on the joints and muscles and other soft tissues, gradually increasing their flexibility. They should be carried out gently to avoid strain. Suitable exercises, depending on your capability, include shoulder shrugging and simple back and neck movements. These exercises are described in more detail on pages 80–81 and 100–101.

Probably one of the easiest ways of achieving an effective cardiovascular warm-up is by brisk walking or marching on the spot, swinging your arms and raising your knees high, for three to five minutes. Your heart rate and breathing will increase and you will also work the main muscle groups and joints of your limbs and back. This can then be followed by the more specific stretching exercises mentioned above.

left *Brisk walking on the spot is an ideal cardiovascular warm-up exercise.*

far left *Exercise stimulates heart and breathing rates and increases blood flow to the muscles.*

THE VALUE OF EXERCISE

WHY STRETCH?

For back-pain sufferers stretching is particularly important because pain is usually associated with a degree of tension or spasm in the back muscles. This in turn will reduce the mobility of the painful part of the back, placing additional strain on the unaffected parts of the spine. Stretching exercises are designed to ease tight muscles, thereby increasing the range of movement in that part of the body.

Stretching exercises can also help keep your back in good condition. If your joints are able to move freely and easily, then you can undertake a greater variety of everyday tasks without the risk of strain. Increasing stiffness in the spine is common as we grow older, but it is not inevitable. The regular practice of stretching exercises helps your body retain its youthful suppleness for longer. Stretching is also an important part of any daily exercise programme because it helps reduce the risk of injury while you are exercising and prevent post-activity stiffness.

above Some stretches can be done while seated on a chair, which may be useful in a work situation or for those with reduced mobility.

right Gentle stretching exercises help to keep your back in good condition.

Stretching and posture

For those with back trouble, stretching exercises for the spine have a particular benefit. Bad postural habits can result in contraction and stiffening of certain back muscles and ligaments, maintaining the postural fault. By gradually stretching these tissues, you can help your body to adopt a healthier and more balanced posture, which will mean that your back is under less strain.

When and how to stretch

Stretching exercises should be done immediately after your warm-up exercises and at the end of a session. They should not be done when your muscles are 'cold' as this could result in strain of the muscles and ligaments. Injuries are most likely when you try to perform an exercise hurriedly, so make sure that you are relaxed and have plenty of time. Never 'bounce' in and out of a stretch as this can cause injury.

How far to stretch

Instructions for a variety of stretching exercises are given in the exercise sections. They should all be performed slowly and precisely. You can maintain your present degree of flexibility by regularly taking each joint to the point where you begin to feel a slight tension in the associated muscles. To improve your

left *The hips and thighs can also benefit from gentle stretching.*

flexibility, however, you need to hold the position and maintain the stretch for ten seconds or more so that the muscle gradually relaxes.

You will need to distinguish between the not unpleasant sensation of stretching and the warning signs of discomfort or even pain. There is no added benefit in taking a stretch beyond the point where it is comfortable. Pain is a sign of impending or actual injury and a signal to stop the exercise.

Breathing

For effective stretching it is helpful to be aware of your breathing. Always breathe regularly and deeply as you are performing a stretch to ensure maximum relaxation. Generally you should exhale as you start the stretch. Never hold your breath while stretching as this creates unnecessary tension and may counteract the benefits of the exercise.

THE VALUE OF EXERCISE

WHY STRENGTHEN?

Strengthening exercises for the back and abdominal muscles are the cornerstones of an effective exercise programme for back problems. Many people who suffer from back trouble have weakened muscles in the back and abdomen and this can often be both a cause and an effect of poor postural habits. Good tone in the abdominal muscles is vital for a healthy back. Improving the strength of the back and abdominal muscles helps support the spine and reduces strain on the joints and ligaments. Strong back and abdominal muscles also help prevent injury to the spine when performing physical tasks such as lifting and carrying.

What are strengthening exercises?

Most types of strengthening exercises involve using the muscles to exert a force against resistance. For some forms of exercises that resistance may be provided by weights. For the abdominal and back strengthening exercises in this book, the resistance used is that of the weight of the body itself.

There are two types of strengthening exercise: toning and building. When toning muscles, they are worked repeatedly against relatively low resistance and this increases strength and endurance without much increase in muscle

below left *Back-strengthening exercises should always start with a small range of movement.*

below right *Over time, the range of movement can slowly be enhanced.*

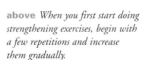

above *When you first start doing strengthening exercises, begin with a few repetitions and increase them gradually.*

bulk. In muscle building, the muscles are worked against greater resistance (heavier weights) for fewer repetitions and this increases muscle bulk and the capacity for exerting a high degree of force for a short period. For strengthening back and abdominal muscles, toning exercises are the most beneficial and are therefore the ones that are described in this book.

When you first start to do strengthening exercises you will probably find that you are only able to do a few repetitions without tiring and you are likely to need frequent rests. This is not an indication of laziness or lack of commitment; it is a physiological necessity. Modern fitness instructors and back-care practitioners advise strongly against the idea of 'going for the burn', that is, continuing to work aching muscles. When your muscles start to ache or suddenly become weak or shaky, it is time to stop that exercise for that session. As your muscles become stronger you will be able to increase the number of repetitions that you can do.

After any exercise, but in particular strengthening exercises, it is very important to do some cool-down stretches, preferably followed by a period of relaxation, however brief. If you omit the stretch stage your muscles will invariably feel stiff and ache the next day, and the risk of subsequent injury is increased.

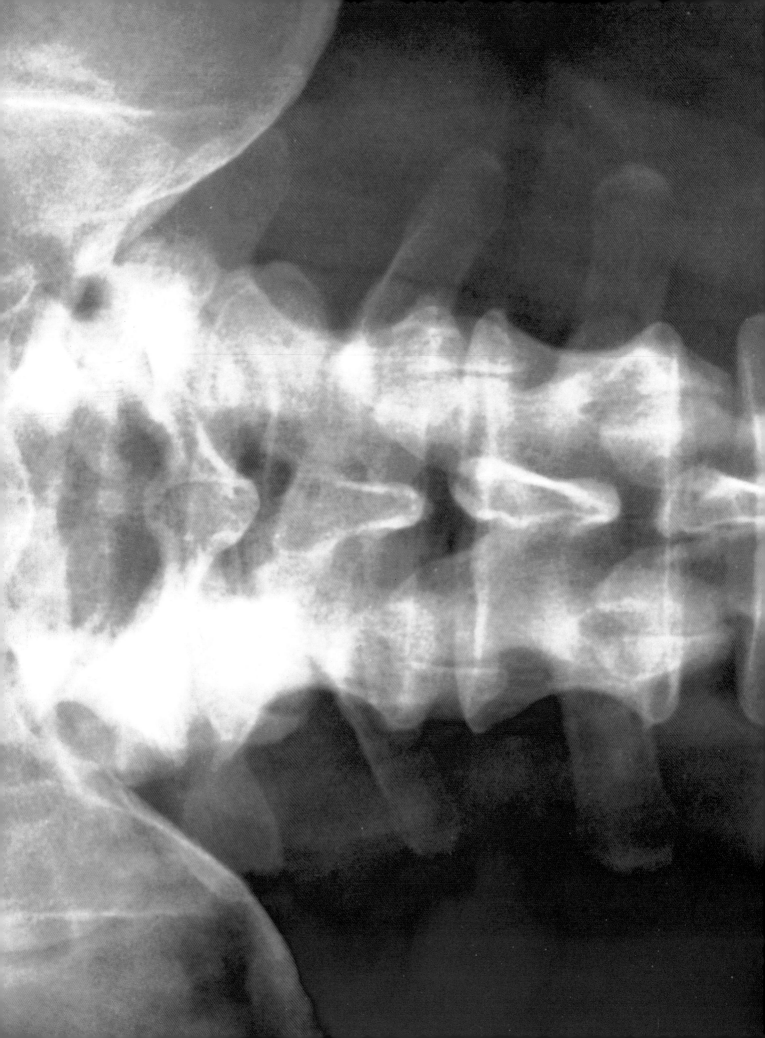

3

ASSESSING
YOUR CONDITION

HOW SERIOUS IS YOUR PROBLEM?

When you are suffering from back pain, the first priority is to assess the severity and possible cause of your problem. This is important in deciding what action you can take for yourself or whether you need to seek the advice and help of a doctor, osteopath or other back-care practitioner. Clearly some back injuries caused by severe trauma carry the risk of fracture of the spine. In such cases, immediate medical attention is required and the person should not be moved until medical assistance has arrived.

It is also important to consider the possibility of a non-spinal cause of back pain. Occasionally certain conditions affecting the internal organs can also cause pain in the back. These include kidney infections and gynaecological problems, such as pelvic inflammatory disease or endometriosis. In such cases, you may experience other symptoms in addition to having pain in the back. If you are unwell and also experiencing severe back pain it is therefore important that you consult your doctor.

Chronic back trouble can also be an indicator of a serious condition. For this reason you should always consult your doctor or back-care practitioner if there is any change in the nature or severity of your symptoms or if they fail to improve after a few weeks of self-help action.

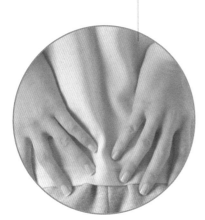

Acute or chronic?

If this is the first time you have experienced this particular back problem or it represents a recent, severe flare-up of a previous back problem, then for the purpose of initial management it should be considered an acute problem. In this case, follow the checklist and advice opposite *(top)*.

If, however, these symptoms are not new to you, but have been troubling you in more or less the same way and with much the same degree of severity for several months or more, then it can probably be considered a chronic problem. In this case go directly to the checklist and advice opposite *(far right)*.

ASSESSING A BACK PROBLEM

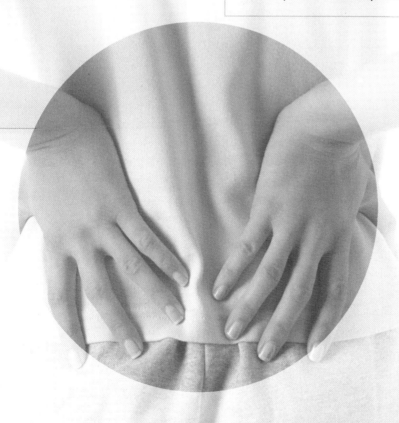

Consult your doctor at once if you are experiencing acute back pain and if:

- Pain follows an injury or fall and you also have pain or numbness in, or difficulty moving, an arm or a leg.
- You have impaired, or loss of, bladder control.
- You have a fever, feel generally unwell and have a severe headache or other symptoms, such as a change in bowel habit.
- You are over 60 or have been immobilized by illness or injury or taking steroids for many years.
- You have chest pain or pain in your left arm.
- You are pregnant.

If none of the above applies to you, try the immediate action measures recommended on pages 52–53 before progressing to the Stage 1 exercises in Part Four *(see page 65)*. Consult your back-care practitioner for an assessment of your back as soon as you are reasonably mobile.

Get advice from your doctor for chronic back pain if:

- Your symptoms suddenly get worse (see also the advice for acute pain).
- You have been losing weight without intending to.
- You have been feeling below par and generally unwell.
- You experience difficulty moving, or have unusual sensations in your arms or legs.
- You have problems moving your bowels or with urination.
- You have been experiencing increasing and significant stiffness as well as pain.
- You have not yet had an expert diagnosis of your back problem.

If none of the above applies, you are ready to start the Stage 1 back exercises *(see page 65)* once you have read the rest of this chapter.

IMMEDIATE ACTION

An attack of acute back pain can be severe and disabling. It may immediately follow a strain, such as lifting an excessively heavy load or a fall. Sometimes, however, the effects of the injury may not become apparent until you wake the following morning and experience difficulty in getting out of bed because of pain and stiffness. In either case, after having checked the cautions on page 51, there are several measures you can take to help relieve your symptoms and prepare yourself for an exercise programme to speed recovery.

In general, any period of rest following an acute back problem should not last for more than 24–48 hours. Even during this time try to encourage, if the pain allows, some movement in your back – you may be able to do a gentle knee hug *(see page 72)* lying on your side. Once the pain has abated so that you can undertake a greater variety of movements, you can start to mobilize your back with some gentle exercises *(see pages 80–81)*. An early return to normal activities reduces the risk of your problem becoming a chronic condition.

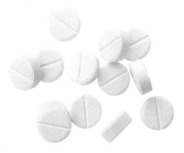

above *Medication, in the form of analgesic and anti-inflammatory drugs, can be helpful in relieving back pain.*

below *Find a position that feels comfortable and that eases your pain.*

Rest positions

When acute back strain first strikes, taking the pressure off your spine, especially if a disc injury is suspected, is usually necessary. Ideally you need to lie down, as this removes downward gravitational pressure on the disc and allows your muscles to relax more easily. Preferably lie on a bed, as the floor does not provide sufficient support and is more difficult to get up from. Sometimes, sitting supported in a chair is more comfortable, so be guided by what feels best. Never remain in a position that increases your pain. Try to change your position regularly, avoiding sudden painful movements. As soon as you can, get up to walk around for a few minutes every hour.

Your choice of position

It is important that you choose a position that provides maximum relaxation of every area of your spine. Lying flat on your back with support in key areas is often most comfortable. However, for some people other positions offer better relaxation and greater pain relief, so adopt whatever position gives you most relief.

If you choose to lie down, place a pillow under your head and neck if you wish. Bend your knees and place one or more pillows under your knees for support, or rest your lower legs on a footstool or seat of a chair so that your legs are bent at a right-angle. This position allows your lumbar curve to flatten towards the bed or floor, gently stretching your back muscles. If your back is still hurting, you may find that placing a small rolled-up

above *The application of an ice pack to the painful area can often be beneficial.*

towel in the small of your back (under the lumbar spine) helps to reduce the pain. If you are uncomfortable on your back, try lying on your side, knees curled up towards your chest so that your spine is flexed. Less commonly, you may find relief from pain by lying on your front with a pillow under your waist so that your back is slightly arched.

Pain-relieving medication

Although pain is useful in alerting us to injury or disease, there is no need to put up with continuing pain when it can often be alleviated by appropriate medication.

Several over-the-counter medications are effective for acute back pain. Non-steroidal anti-inflammatory drugs (NSAIDs) such as ibuprofen – alone or with codeine phosphate – may be a better choice than paracetamol because they are anti-inflammatory as well as pain-relieving. Do not take these medications without the advice of your doctor if you have a history of asthma or stomach ulcers, and discontinue them if you feel any stomach discomfort. Always read the precautions on the package and do not exceed the recommended dose. Preparations containing codeine will have a slight constipating effect. To counteract this drink plenty of water and increase your fibre intake.

If over-the-counter medications do not provide adequate relief, consult your doctor, who may prescribe more powerful medication and possibly a short course of muscle-relaxant drugs if your back is in severe spasm.

Hot and cold

The use of heat and cold in the relief of aches and pains is simple and effective. The application of a covered hot-water bottle or heated pad can help to relax tense, painful muscles. It is advisable to apply a cold pack for a minute or two after the heat. Acute back pain, however, often responds better to cold, which reduces inflammation and swelling, so try placing a packet of frozen peas, wrapped in a cloth, against the most painful area, or buy a gel pack designed for this purpose.

Alternating cold and hot is usually the most successful method for relieving back pain and muscle spasm. Using a covered cold pack and hot-water bottle, first apply the cold pack to the painful area. After a minute or two apply the hot pack for the same time, then the cold, the hot and finally the cold. Always start and end on cold and repeat the treatment every few hours.

Relaxation

Much of the pain from an acute back strain may come from the muscle spasm that follows the injury. Having found a position in which you can rest physically, try to concentrate on relaxing the painful muscles. Breathe in through your nose for a slow count of four; hold your breath for a count of three, then breathe out fully through your mouth for a count of six. On the out-breaths try to let the tension in your body disperse, starting with your head and jaw and working down your body, arms and legs to your toes. Do this for several minutes as often as you can. Other relaxation techniques *(see pages 75 and 139)* may also be of benefit.

PREPARATION FOR EXERCISE

For many people who suffer an acute attack of back pain it is the culmination of years of a generally sedentary lifestyle, poor posture and numerous minor strains and injuries. Your recovery exercise programme therefore needs to be carefully planned so that you learn new ways of looking after your back that can become second nature. It is also important to ensure that you grade your programme according to your capabilities so that you do not strain yourself by being overambitious at the outset. Be prepared to adapt your routine if you find it too strenuous, if pain increases or returns, or additional symptoms occur.

A programme for life

A successful exercise programme is one that you enjoy and that fits in easily with your daily routine. Therefore spend some time planning your exercise schedule, but be realistic and accept that sometimes you really will be too busy to exercise or may feel unwell. Your exercise programme is personal to you, and you should not judge your capabilities and progress according to what others might be able to achieve. We are all different, so do not force your body into positions for which it is not yet ready or ones that it will never be able to achieve!

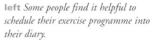

left Some people find it helpful to schedule their exercise programme into their diary.

Get advice

If you are in any doubt at all
concerning the suitability of your
exercise programme, make sure that
you consult your doctor or back-
care practitioner, who will be able to
give you expert advice on whether
or not you should proceed with it.
This is particularly important if
you have undergone spinal surgery
at any time.

above *Check with your back-care
practitioner or doctor if you have any
doubts about embarking on an
exercise programme.*

CAUTION

LISTEN TO YOUR BODY AND BE PREPARED TO
ADAPT YOUR PROGRAMME FROM DAY TO DAY IF
NECESSARY. THE WAY WE FEEL CAN VARY A GREAT
DEAL AND WHAT WAS EASY ON ONE DAY MAY SEEM
DIFFICULT OR UNCOMFORTABLE ON ANOTHER.
THEREFORE MODIFY YOUR EXERCISE PROGRAMME
TO WHAT SEEMS RIGHT FOR YOU AT THE TIME.

ASSESSING YOUR CONDITION

BODY AWARENESS

Most of us take our body for granted, giving little thought to the effects of all the physical demands we make on it, until such time as we suffer pain or injury. One of the benefits of regular exercise is that you learn to become more aware of your body and can adapt your activities to create greater physical harmony. Exercise performed without body awareness carries a higher risk of injury and is less likely to be performed effectively. To develop body awareness you need to be mentally focused so that you can give your full attention to any exercise or movement you are doing.

right *Exercise helps to develop a greater awareness of your body.*

Start relaxed, stay relaxed

Before you begin the exercises in this book, check your posture *(see pages 98–99)* and run through the following checklist so that your body is free from any unconscious signs of tension and strain:

- Soften your gaze so that your eyes are not rigidly focused on any one object.
- Check that your breathing is slow, regular and deep.
- Relax your shoulders, taking care not to be round-shouldered or to force your shoulders back unnaturally.
- Relax your mouth and jaw so that your lips are slightly parted and your teeth are not clenched tightly together.
- Lengthen your spine upwards as if you were being pulled gently from the top of your head,

remembering to keep your pelvis tilted correctly *(see page 66).*

- Soften your knees and elbows *(see page 58).*

Repeat these checks during your exercise session. After a while they should become automatic.

Listening to your body

Constantly be aware of how your body is responding to the demands of each exercise that you undertake. Does the movement cause you any discomfort? Is the sensation that you are feeling a pleasant stretch or could you be straining yourself? Is the ache in your muscles a sign that they are being worked effectively or an indication that you are overdoing it and should stop?

The golden rule is that you should always stop an exercise if you think that the sensations that you are feeling could be warning you of a potential injury. No harm will come from being overcautious, but you could risk all the progress you have achieved by ignoring vital warning signs. You can always attempt the exercise again in a few days' time, but be prepared to stop if it does not feel comfortable.

Conscious movement

Controlled movement is the aim of every exercise in this book. Throughout the exercise section you will be reminded to tense your abdominal muscles to protect your lower back from injury and to tilt your pelvis to its correct position. Every movement you make while doing an exercise should be carried out in a conscious and careful way. Injury can occur when you lose control of a movement and let momentum rather than muscle control take over.

above *Even when you are not exercising, try to be aware of – and control – your movements.*

JOINT CARE

Keep in mind the need to care for your joints during exercise. Weight-bearing joints, such as the knees, are at particular risk if they are not properly aligned as specified in the instructions for each exercise, so always check that they are correctly positioned before you start.

Knees are hinge joints that allow the legs to be bent and straightened, permitting only a small degree of rotation movement. Rotation of the knee when weight-bearing can overstretch or even damage the ligaments, so make sure you keep your knees facing forward during exercise. For maximum protection of all your joints, always move gently and in complete control into and out of a particular exercise position, aiming to make all movements flowing and rhythmical. Never 'bounce' movement through a joint, as this can cause a severe strain injury. If you experience any pain in a particular joint while exercising, stop the exercise immediately.

top right *Take particular care to support your neck while you are exercising.*

Keeping joints 'soft'

When a joint is held locked in a rigid, straight, fully extended position, it is unable to absorb the shocks created by movements of the body. This can cause jarring and strain of that joint. A 'soft' joint is held in a slightly flexed position that prepares it for movement. During standing exercises your knees should be slightly flexed to prevent any jarring of the spine and damage to the knee joints. Elbows should be soft in any exercise in which they support the weight of the body – for example in the kneeling-stretch exercise on pages 120–121.

Neck care

Neck strain is one of the most
common problems that can come
about as a result of an incorrect
exercise technique.

As the neck is anatomically part
of the spine it needs to be kept in
balance with the rest of the back
when you are standing. If the
weight of the head shifts away from
the midline, then tension in the
supporting muscles and ligaments
of the cervical spine may result
in discomfort.

Whenever possible, therefore,
aim to keep the neck 'long' and the
weight of the head and neck aligned
with the rest of the spine so that
pressure is evenly distributed.
Follow the specific instructions
on positioning the head and neck
that are given for each exercise.

In some of the abdominal
strengthening exercises the neck is
potentially at risk from strain. If
you find that your neck muscles are
feeling uncomfortable, either during
or after exercise, then you could
consider buying a relatively cheap
and easily available piece of exercise
equipment. This supports your head
and neck in the correct position
while you strengthen your
abdominal muscles.

*left When standing, the head and
neck should be held comfortably
balanced in line with the spine.*

MENTAL FOCUS

Even the most simple of exercises requires complete concentration to obtain the maximum benefit. Therefore try to arrange your exercise time so that you are unlikely to be disturbed or distracted. Do not be tempted to listen to the radio or play music while you are learning your exercises, but once you have mastered them, playing relaxing classical or new-age music that does not have a strong set tempo or beat may make your exercise session more enjoyable.

While some forms of dance-related exercise, such as aerobics, use music in order to help provide rhythm and pace, this is not appropriate for the specific exercises that are described in this book. You need to set your own rhythm according to your own ability and your personal energy levels. When music is being played there is generally a temptation to match your tempo to that of the music. This can result in reduced attention being paid to the accuracy of your movements, possibly resulting in strain.

above *Many Eastern forms of exercise and meditation, such as t'ai chi, require mental focus and concentration on your breathing.*

Breathing

Oxygen extracted from the air we breathe is essential for the production of energy to power our muscles; it is also required in greater-than-normal amounts during exercise. When we breathe out, we expel carbon dioxide, a waste product of energy production, which is increased during exercise. It is therefore important while you are exercising to pay attention to your breathing and to ensure that you work in a warm but well-ventilated room.

Many of those who are new to exercise concentrate so hard on performing the actual movements accurately that they literally forget to breathe! Holding your breath deprives the body of vital oxygen and causes unnecessary muscle tension and fatigue. Whichever exercise you are performing, make sure that you breathe in and out slowly and regularly throughout the various movements.

The instructions for certain exercises specify when you should breathe in and/or out. Be sure to follow this guidance in order to gain maximum benefit from the exercises in question.

You can improve your awareness, both of your own breathing and of your mental focus, by practising the following extremely simple breathing exercise:

1 Lie on your back on your bed or a soft surface on the floor, with your knees bent and your feet on the floor, hip width apart. Place a small cushion under your head and neck for support, if you wish.

2 Rest your hands on your abdomen, palms down, so that your thumbs are on your lowest ribs and your fingers fan out on either side of your navel, with the fingertips just touching when you have breathed out fully. You may find you can concentrate better if you close your eyes.

3 Now take a deep breath in through your nose, feeling the air fill your lungs from the very bottom where your thumbs are resting. This should have the

effect of distending your abdomen upwards and outwards so that the space between your fingertips increases by several centimetres. Keep on filling your lungs with air until even the very top lobes of your lungs, just under your collar bones, are full.

4 Now breathe out slowly and deliberately, expelling the air through your mouth until your lungs are as empty as you can make them.

5 Repeat this exercise at least another five times. It is an excellent, quick and simple way to relieve stress. It can also be practised while you are sitting in a chair, once you have mastered the technique.

below left *During inhalation the diaphragm contracts, moving downwards and inflating the lungs. The chest and abdomen expand.*

below *During expiration the diaphragm relaxes and moves upwards, deflating the lungs, while the chest and abdomen relax.*

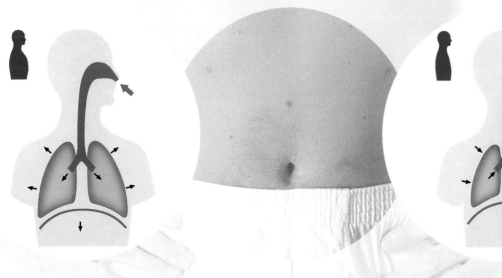

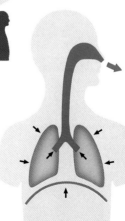

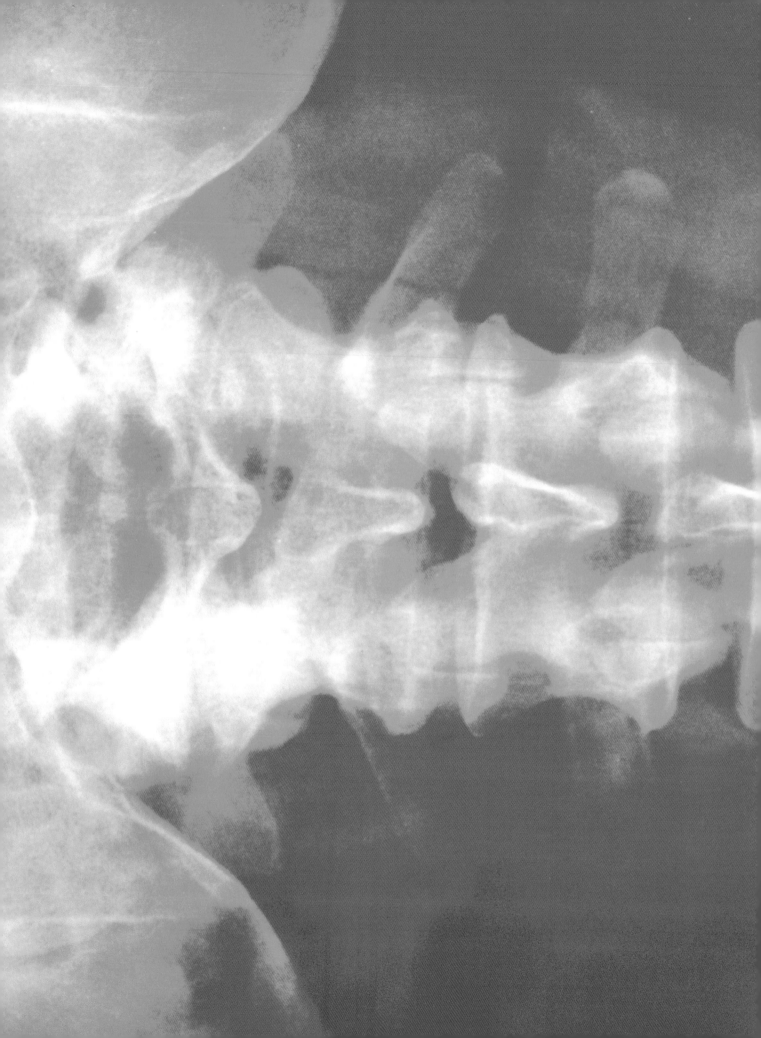

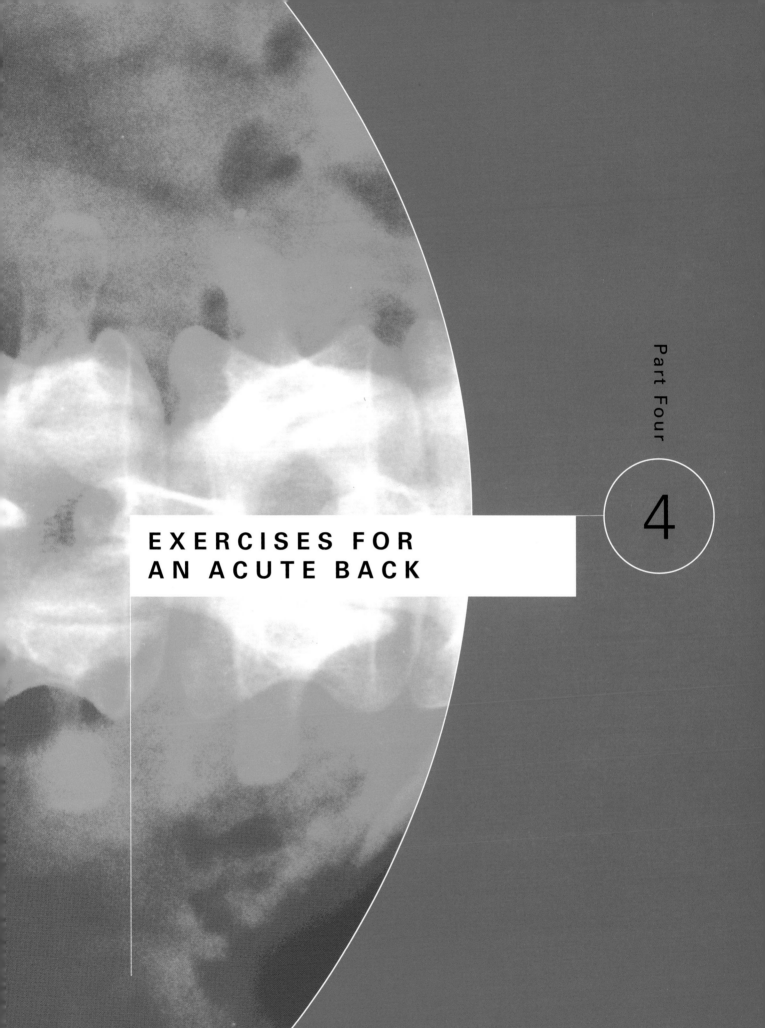

4

EXERCISES FOR
AN ACUTE BACK

INTRODUCTION

EXERCISES FOR AN ACUTE BACK

These are exercises designed for people who are currently suffering from pain and stiffness in the back. If the pain came on suddenly or is new for you, it is assumed that you will have followed the advice in Part Three. Remember that if you are in any doubt as to whether you should exercise or not then you should consult your doctor or other back-care practitioner. The following exercises should also form the first stage of your back-exercise programme if you are new to exercise or have not exercised for a long time.

The aim of the exercises is to encourage mobility, reduce muscle spasm and speed recovery. They include a technique that is fundamental to most of the exercises in this book; the pelvic tilt. All readers, whatever their level of fitness, should make a special point of familiarizing themselves with this technique. It is the basis of good posture and safe back exercising.

Which exercises, how often and in what order?

Your exercise schedule will depend on the severity of your condition and how quickly you make progress. Remember that there is no benefit in overworking your back at this stage – a strain incurred through doing too much too soon could set back your recovery. Everyone responds at a different pace so, if in doubt, err on the side of caution.

Acute back problems

1 If you are experiencing, or just recovering from, an acute back problem and need to rest lying down for some of the time, begin with the lying pelvic tilt *(see page 67)* and the knee hugging *(see page 72)*. Do a few repeats every hour or so. Little and often is the key. Try to practise total relaxation *(see pages 74–75)* twice per day.

2 As your symptoms improve (in most cases usually within a day or so) and you can move more easily, add the seated spinal stretch *(see page 69)* and possibly gently try the leg rolling *(see page 73)*. Do the seated spinal stretch, pelvic

tilt and knee hugging every hour or so and the leg rolling three times a day, provided that it does not aggravate your back pain. Continue with your twice-daily relaxation session.

3 When the pain has abated further and mobility in your back has improved, try the remaining exercises in this section. Do a balanced selection of exercises, ideally three times a day. For example, one form of pelvic tilt, one spinal stretch and one spinal rotation *(see sample programme right)*. Practise relaxation once or twice a day. Maintain this exercise regime for at least one week before moving on to the exercises in Part Five.

A
- Lying pelvic tilt *(see page 67)*
- Knee hugging *(see page 72)*
- Relaxation *(see pages 74–75)*

B
- Lying pelvic tilt *(see page 67)*
- Knee hugging *(see page 72)*
- Leg rolling *(see page 73)*
- Seated spinal stretch *(see page 69)*
- Relaxation *(see pages 74–75)*

C
- Pelvic tilts: standing *(see page 66)*, sitting *(see page 68)* or lying *(see page 67)*
- Spinal stretches: seated spinal stretch *(see page 69)*, seated spinal rotation *(see page 70)*, seated side-stretch *(see page 71)*
- Knee hugging *(see page 72)*
- Leg rolling *(see page 73)*
- Relaxation *(see pages 74–75)*

Newcomers to exercise

If you are unaccustomed to exercise you should work your way through the staged exercise programme given above. You may, however, find that you are able to progress more quickly through Stages A and B. Like those with an acute back problem, practise the Stage C routine for at least a week before progressing further.

THE PELVIC TILT

Maintaining a correct pelvic tilt and keeping your abdominal muscles gently tensed whenever you do an exercise protects your spine from injury and ensures that you are doing the exercises effectively. When learning the exercises it may be helpful to think of the pelvis *(see page 19)* as a bowl. Imagine it filled with water and that, when your pelvis is tilted correctly, the fluid is contained within the bowl. However, by tilting the bowl either forwards or backwards (incorrectly), the fluid may flow over the edge.

STANDING PELVIC TILT

Use this exercise to observe what an improvement the correct pelvic tilt makes to your posture. You can watch yourself in a mirror to see the difference that it makes.

WATCHPOINT

● When you tense your abdominal muscles, make it a gradual movement, concentrating on slowly drawing the muscle below your navel back towards your spine. This cannot be achieved with a sudden movement. If you are tensing your abdominal muscles correctly there should be no (or only minimal) change in your lower ribcage. When you relax your abdominal muscles, make this movement slow and controlled, too. Remember that these muscles support the spine and provide it with vital protection while doing any exercise.

1 Incorrect pelvic tilt

Stand upright with your weight evenly distributed and your knees very slightly flexed so that your knee joints are not locked. Imagine that you are being pulled gently upwards, and slightly forwards, by an invisible thread attached to the top of your head. Place one hand on your stomach just below your navel and the other hand so that the heel is in the small of your back and your fingers are pointing down, covering your sacrum. Hollow your back and feel your pelvis tilt incorrectly, with your sacrum moving from the vertical towards the horizontal plane. Note how your stomach pushes out against your hand.

LYING PELVIC TILT

Having perfected tilting your pelvis while you are standing, you can now try it while lying down. If you are currently suffering from acute low back pain, only attempt step 2.

① **Back arched**

Lie on the ground with your head supported on a cushion if you wish. Place your hands above you or beside you – wherever they feel comfortable. Gently arch your back, creating a hollow in the small of your back by slackening your abdominal muscles and tilting your pelvis incorrectly. Do not perform this part of the exercise if it causes any discomfort in your back.

② **Back flattened**

Now contract your abdominal muscles and tilt your pelvis the correct way so that the hollow disappears and your lower back is in contact with the floor. Repeat this sequence slowly until you are confident that you know just how it feels to create the correct pelvic tilt. This is also an exercise to gently stretch the lower back and to increase mobility.

② **Correct pelvic tilt**

Now roll your pelvis the other way and feel your abdomen pull in, the hollow in your back flatten and the bottom of your sacrum tuck downwards and forwards. This is the correct pelvic tilt and it is possible to maintain it whether you are standing, sitting or lying down. With practice it will become a habit always to tilt your pelvis in this way. Practise the wrong and then the correct way of holding your pelvis, monitoring the movement with your hands. Then take your hands away and practise a few more times.

SITTING PELVIC TILT

Throughout the sitting exercises you will be asked to tilt your pelvis correctly. It is always as well to tilt your pelvis routinely to improve your sitting posture and reduce the strain on your lower back. The use of a back support, cushion or a small rolled towel placed in the lower lumbar area may improve your comfort, especially when your back is particularly painful.

Pelvic tilting as an exercise

When you have perfected the pelvic tilt it can be used as an exercise to stretch the muscles of your lower back. Gently and slowly roll from the incorrect to the correct tilt five times, holding the correct position for ten seconds. Always finish in the correct tilting position. This exercise can be very helpful after a long car journey or if you have been standing still for too long.

Pelvis forward   1

To learn how to tilt your pelvis correctly when sitting, choose a firm chair or a stool. Sit with both your feet on the floor, hip-width apart (and your back in contact with the back of the chair, if you are using one). Draw in your abdominal muscles and sit up tall, imagining that you are being pulled gently upwards from the top of your head. Now roll your pelvis forward so that your back arches. It may help to remember the 'bowl of fluid' example *(see page 66)*. In this position the fluid would flow over the front of the bowl.

2   Pelvis back

Now roll your pelvis in the opposite direction, so that the imaginary bowl is level and the fluid is contained within it. If you were to roll your pelvis too far back, however, the fluid would once again spill out.

WATCHPOINT

● When tensing your abdominal muscles remember that any movement of your lower ribs should be inwards and downwards, rather than forcing them upwards and outwards.

SEATED STRETCHES

The seated exercises provide good, simple stretches for the entire spine, helping to maintain its flexibility. It is important to keep the abdominal muscles gently tensed throughout these exercises *(see Watchpoint on page 66)*.

SEATED SPINAL STRETCH

This exercise, when done correctly, provides an excellent gentle stretch for the whole spine, particularly the lower back. However, it is very easy to do it incorrectly, so follow the instructions carefully and concentrate! Do this exercise frequently during the day.

Body erect ①

Sit towards the front of a firm chair or stool with your legs slightly apart. Sit tall and gently tense your abdominal muscles. Rest your hands on your thighs, or let them hang between your legs as you become more flexible.

WATCHPOINT

● If your back is acutely painful you might find that just flexing your head and upper back forward and down is sufficient to achieve a stretching sensation in your lower back. Rest your hands on your thighs and use your arms to gently lever you upright again.

② Body curled

Now, keeping your abdominal muscles gently tensed, start by bending your chin towards your chest and slowly curl forward, imagining your spine slowly flexing and opening, vertebra by vertebra, until you are flexed right down to your last lumbar vertebra. This movement should take you at least ten seconds. Keep your pelvis still, being careful not to rock forward through your hip joints. Remember to keep breathing throughout the exercise and relax into the stretch without letting your abdominal muscles slacken. Once you have flexed as far as you feel comfortable, enjoy the sensation of stretch throughout your spine for 10–20 seconds before uncurling very slowly, coming upright to sit tall again. Do not repeat the exercise immediately, but practise it several times throughout the day.

SEATED SPINAL ROTATION

This is a good exercise to stretch your spine, gently improving your mobility. It can be done quickly and easily several times during the day. Build up gradually from one to five repetitions.

1 Left shoulder forward

Sit upright on a stool or towards the front of a firm chair. Imagine your spine lengthening as if you were being pulled gently upwards from the top of your head. Rest your hands on your shoulders with your elbows out to the sides. Tense your abdominal muscles and tilt your pelvis correctly. Now, without moving your pelvis, very slowly turn to your right by pushing your left shoulder forward; at the same time and with the same amount of pressure, pull your right shoulder back behind you. Breathe in as you turn. Imagine that, as you begin to turn, the rotational movement is starting in the vertebrae in your upper back (not your neck) and slowly spreading down your spine to your lower back. Do not move your pelvis on the seat.

2 Increasing the rotation

Continue to rotate as far as you can with comfort. Hold for a count of ten, then slowly untwist to the starting position and rotate to your left.

WATCHPOINTS

● To avoid straining your neck, make your shoulder tip lead the way, keeping your head in a neutral position between your shoulders.
● Do not force the turn. You should only twist as far as you can with ease. You will probably find that you can turn further to one side. Do not try to force the movement on the restricted side.

SEATED SIDE-STRETCH

This is another very useful exercise to help improve the mobility in your back. As with the other seated exercises, it is vitally important that you keep your abdominal muscles tensed throughout and only take the movement as far as is comfortable for you. This exercise can be repeated several times during the day, adding more repetitions as your back improves, to a maximum of five.

1 Leaning to the left

Choose a firm chair without arms or a stool. Sit with both feet on the floor, your abdominal muscles tensed and your pelvis tilted correctly. Draw yourself upwards to lengthen your spine and allow your hands to rest at your sides, shoulders relaxed, keeping your head and neck straight. Very gradually start to lean to the left, beginning the movement with your left shoulder moving towards the floor. Starting at the mid-thoracic level (between the shoulderblades), imagine your spine bending to the left, slowly working down to your lumbar vertebrae. Your pelvis should not tip as you move, and take care not to twist your spine. You might find it helpful to breathe out as you stretch down and breathe in as you come to the upright position. Stretch only as far as feels comfortable.

2 Leaning to the right

Return to the upright position, remembering not to relax your abdominal muscles. Then repeat the exercise leaning to the right.

EXERCISES

LOWER BACK EXERCISES

These exercises help to stretch the muscles of the lower back and ease any tension there. If you have a very painful back you will not be able to bring your knees as close to your chest as shown; only hug them as far as is comfortable.

KNEE HUGGING

This is an extremely useful exercise to try when you have sustained a recent back strain and your back muscles are feeling particularly tight and movements are painful and restricted. If you have been resting in bed because of back pain, do this exercise regularly, especially before you try to get up, as it will provide a good stretch for your lower back muscles and will prepare them for the increased effort required in rising.

WATCHPOINT

● If grasping around your knees hurts them, try grasping behind your knees, holding the backs of your thighs.

1 Pelvis tilted
Lie on your back, preferably supporting your head on a cushion or pillow. Bend your knees and place your feet, hip-width apart, as shown. Slowly pull in your abdominal muscles to protect your spine and then gently tilt your pelvis to the correct position. Now imagine the lower part of your sacrum being pulled towards your knees and feel your lumbar vertebrae gently pressing down against the surface that you are lying on.

2 One knee to chest
Now bring your left knee up to your chest and grasp it with your hands. Slowly pull the leg towards your chest as far as you can without discomfort; hold for five seconds. Then slowly lower it to the starting position. Repeat with your right leg.

LEG ROLLING

This exercise gently stretches your lower back muscles and, providing it is done slowly and gradually, is very useful when your back muscles are tight and painful. However, do not attempt it if you have any pain or altered sensations in your legs or feet. It is important that you do not force the roll, stopping as soon as you feel a stretch in your back muscles. Stop immediately if you feel any pain.

Flat on back   1

Lie on your back, head on a cushion if you wish, and stretch your arms out to the sides. Keep your shoulders flat on the ground and bend your knees, keeping your feet on the ground and knees together. Now tilt your pelvis correctly and tense your abdominal muscles.

2   Knees to left

Slowly roll your knees to the left, feeling the stretch spreading up from your hips and into the muscles of your lower back. Keep your shoulders flat on the ground. Allow your knees to roll as far as you find comfortable and, once you have reached that point, try to relax into the stretch while holding your abdominal muscles tensed. Hold for five seconds, remembering to breathe throughout the exercise. Slowly bring your knees back to the starting position and repeat the roll to the right. You may repeat the sequence twice more.

3   Both knees to chest

Now repeat step 2, hugging both knees to your chest. Hold for ten seconds. Feel your lower back gently stretching and lengthening. Remember to breathe! You may repeat this sequence twice more.

RELAXATION

The exercises for an acute back described earlier in this section are deliberately undemanding because they are intended for people who are in the first phase of recovery from an acute back problem or for those who are unaccustomed to exercise. However, some people will find that these exercises are quite physically challenging and others, particularly if they are in the early stages of recovering from an episode of acute back pain, may be feeling tired and stressed. It is therefore important to build into your exercise programme a closing relaxation session to allow any muscular tension to dissipate and to help you feel both physically and mentally refreshed.

You can use the simple relaxation technique described here any time you feel a build-up of stress or tension. Choose a warm, quiet room where you will not be disturbed. Wait at least an hour after eating to allow time to digest the meal before you lie down and relax. Keep your consumption of caffeinated drinks (such as coffee and cola) to a minimum, particularly if you feel irritable or anxious, and do not try to relax for at least an hour after drinking one.

If you are very tired you may find that you drift off to sleep for a while when you are in the relaxation position. This is beneficial because, if your sleep has been disturbed by pain, you need to catch up on it whenever you can. When you are ready to get up, if you have been lying on your back, gently hug your knees to your chest for ten seconds to stretch your lower back. Then gently roll onto your side and stand up slowly. Bear in mind that you might feel a little dizzy or disorientated if you have been deeply relaxed.

RELAXATION POSITION

In order to relax effectively you have to be comfortable so find a position in which you feel as comfortable as possible. If you are taking pain-relieving medication you might find it helpful to plan your relaxation session for an hour or so after you have taken the medication so that you are in less discomfort. You can choose one of the rest positions described on page 52. Make sure that the position you choose allows your breathing to be free and unrestricted. For this reason avoid lying on your front, as this compresses the chest.

Most people find lying on their back comfortable, so lie on a soft but supportive surface with your head and neck resting on a pillow. Bend your knees, keeping both feet flat, hip-width apart, and place a pillow under your knees if you wish. Tilt your pelvis correctly *(see page 66)*, and if the small of your back is still unsupported, place a small towel made into a pad under your back if this feels more comfortable to you. Place your hands with the elbows slightly bent so that they rest comfortably at your sides, or rest them uncrossed on your abdomen *(see page 52),* or cross your arms over your chest, as shown below.

LETTING GO OF TENSION

1 Breathing

In your chosen rest position, close your eyes and relax your face, jaw and lips. Breathe in slowly and deeply through your nose, counting to five as you do so. Hold for a count of three, and then breathe out through your mouth, counting to four or five *(see pages 60–61)*. Focus on your breathing rhythm. Be aware of the breath entering your lungs and expanding your chest and abdomen, and of the out-breath leaving your body as your chest and abdomen relax. Do not force the pace of your breathing.

2 Relaxing the body

Allow your head to relax, with your scalp and jaw loosening, your lips parting slightly and your eyelids becoming so heavy that you have to close them. Allow your vertebrae to sink down, one by one, starting at the top of your neck and moving right down to your pelvis. Allow your shoulders to drop and feel a warmth spreading down your arms to your fingertips. Relax your buttocks and abdomen, allowing your hips to roll outwards. Feel the warmth from your arms spreading through your body and into your legs, flowing right down to your toes. Now enjoy the feeling of deep relaxation for at least ten minutes, breathing easily and rhythmically.

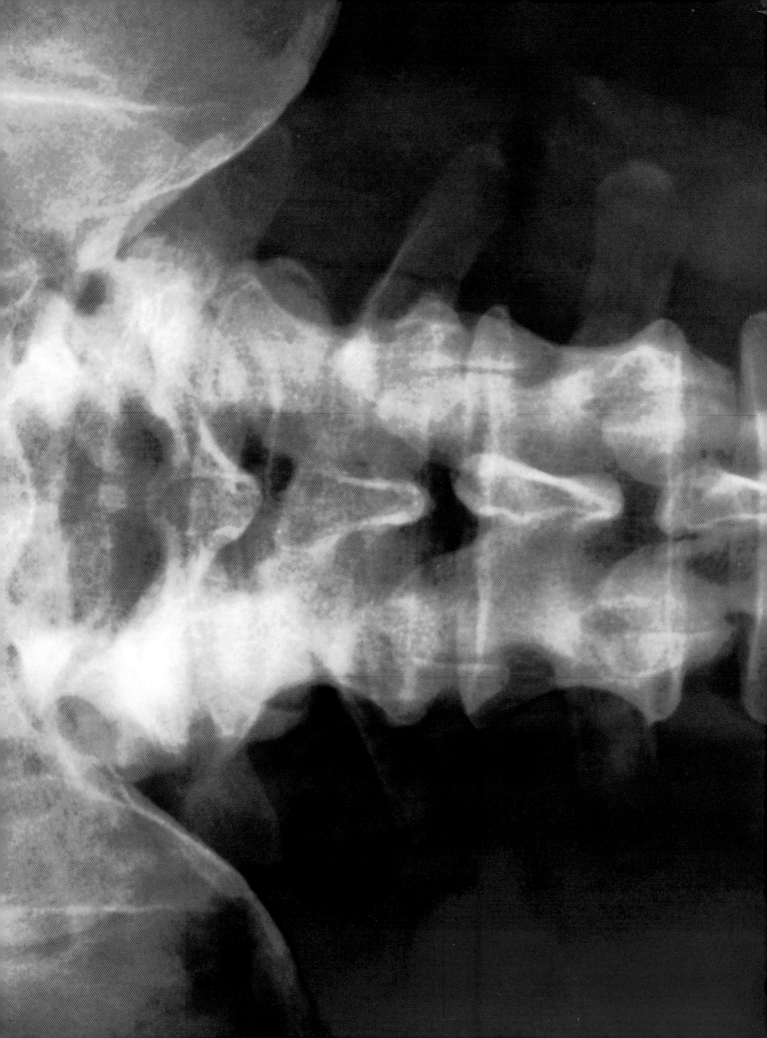

THE RECOVERING BACK

INTRODUCTION

EXERCISES FOR A RECOVERING BACK

Congratulations – you are now on the road to recovery! You can start on this group of exercises when your back pain has improved to the extent that you can move about easily and perform everyday activities with little or no discomfort. You may, however, still be experiencing some stiffness. You will probably need to have been performing the exercises in Part Four for at least a week before moving on to this section. Do not progress to these exercises if you are finding the exercises for an acute back uncomfortable. The aim of exercise at this stage of your recovery is to extend your range of movement by stretching contracted muscles and gradually increasing flexibility. The exercise programme also includes some warm-ups that help to prepare you for stretching. Now is also the time to start increasing your physical activity. Try to walk for at least 20 minutes every day as soon as you are able. Avoid high-impact activities, such as jogging, any sport with a twisting movement such as golf, and any weight-training, until your back is completely recovered.

Don't forget to warm up

Before starting your exercises remember to warm up *(see pages 42–43)*. This should not be too strenuous, but be sufficient to provide a noticeable boost to your heart and breathing rate *(see page 80)*.

Which exercises, how often and in what order?

Your new exercise programme should be seen as an extension of the previous section. You can learn the new exercises one by one and integrate them into a new routine at a pace you feel comfortable with. Having completed your cardiovascular warm-up, do the warm-up stretches *(see pages 80–81)*, a pelvic tilt (when you are ready, learn the kneeling version, *see page 86)*, knee hugging (try the extended version, *see page 83)*, and a spinal rotation *(see, for example, page 88)*. Add further

exercises from this section as you progress. Finish your session with relaxation *(see pages 74–75)*.

Ideally, practise a full routine twice a day. You will need to set aside approximately 15 minutes twice a day plus some relaxation time. If, on some days, this proves impossible do not worry, just do as much as you can, but always find time to do the seated spinal stretch, side-stretch and rotation *(see pages 69–71)* several times during the day. These take only a few minutes to do, but help to prevent you from becoming stiff. Remember, a little exercise is always better than none.

If an exercise causes you pain or discomfort, first check that you are doing it correctly. If it is still uncomfortable, discontinue the exercise and try it again in a few days' time. If it is still uncomfortable, omit it from your programme.

Continue with the exercises in this section until you are confident that you can do the majority of them with ease and without any aggravation of your symptoms either during exercise or the following day. Most people will need to work at this level for at least two weeks before progressing to the more demanding exercises from the Maintenance Programme in Part Six. However, depending on your age, physical condition and particular back problem, you may need to allow yourself more time at this level. Be guided by your body's response to the exercises and, if you are in any doubt, ask your back-care practitioner for advice.

SAMPLE PROGRAMME

Your twice-daily routine should initially comprise exercises from groups A, B, C and D below. You can choose different exercises from within each category to match your ability and to provide variety. You can end with the supine stretch, so that you are in a position ready for relaxation. Add exercises from group E when you feel ready to do so. Remember to warm up before you exercise and to relax afterwards.

A
- Seated spinal stretch *(see page 69)*
- Back stretches *(see page 80)*

B
- Pelvic tilts: standing *(see page 66)*, sitting *(see page 68)*, lying *(see page 67)* or kneeling *(see page 86)*

C
- Knee hugging *(see page 72)*
- Knee hugging with resisted stretch *(see page 83)*

D
- Seated spinal rotation *(see page 70)*
- Seated side-stretch *(see page 71)*
- Leg rolling *(see page 73)*
- Seated rotation in a chair *(see page 88)*
- Seated rotation on the floor *(see page 89)*
- Supine stretch *(see page 91)*

E
- Extended lumbar roll *(see page 84)*
- Prone stretch *(see page 90)*
- Side-shunt *(see page 82)*

GENTLE WARM-UP BACK STRETCHES

Start your exercise session with a gentle warm-up to boost your circulation in preparation for more intensive work. For example, walk on the spot for a few minutes, lifting your knees high and swinging your arms at the same time. Or, if you prefer, take a short, five-minute walk outside. After this general warm-up, do the back stretches that are described below in order to prepare you for further activity.

BACK WARM-UPS

Start this sequence of four stretches by standing tall with your feet positioned hip-width apart. Soften your knees *(see page 58)* and place your hands on your hips. Tilt your pelvis correctly *(see page 66)* and tense your abdominal muscles in order to protect your spine from strain. Return to this same starting position after you have performed each individual exercise and repeat the entire warm-up sequence five times.

WATCHPOINTS

● Discontinue any exercise that causes pain or discomfort.
● Keep your abdominal muscles tensed, but the rest of your body as relaxed as possible.
● Check that you are breathing normally with no tension in your jaw.

1 Flexion

Tuck your chin towards your chest and begin to curl forward slowly, starting with your neck, then upper back, and finally stretching through your lower back. Keep your pelvis tilted correctly *(see page 66)* and your abdominal muscles tensed. Feel the stretch in your back muscles. Hold for ten seconds. Slowly uncurl and return to the starting position.
Note: this is not a toe-touching exercise and you may not need to curl any further forward than shown in the photograph to feel a stretch in your lower back.

2 Rotation

From the starting position slowly turn your trunk to the right, while keeping your pelvis facing forward. Lead the movement with your shoulders, not your head and neck. Turn your head only slightly to the right; if you turn too far you risk straining your neck. Feel the stretch starting in your upper back and extending downwards. Slowly reverse the movement to return to the starting position. Turn to the left.

3 Extension

From the starting position, gently arch your spine backwards. Start the movement with your shoulders. Imagine them being pulled up and back so that your spine lengthens as it bends. Keep your neck relaxed but do not allow your head to tilt back. Keep your pelvis tilted correctly *(see page 66)* and your abdominal muscles tensed to control the extent of the stretch. Do not attempt to arch your spine too far (no further than is shown in the photograph). You should feel a gentle stretch, not tension, strain or pain. Slowly return to the starting position, using your shoulders to lead the movement.

4 Shoulder shrugging

Lift your shoulders slowly up to your ears as you breathe in deeply. Feel your ribcage pulling upwards and your spine lengthening. Hold for a count of three and, while breathing out, slowly drop your shoulders down, stretching them towards your feet. Hold for a count of three and relax into the starting position.

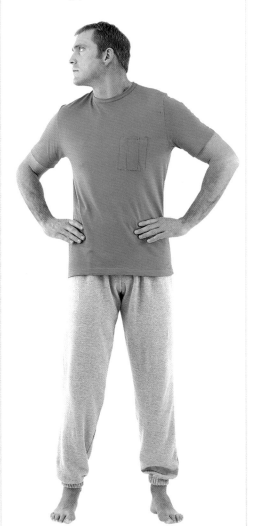

EXERCISES

IMPROVING FLEXIBILITY

The remainder of the exercises in this section focus on stretching your muscles and ligaments in order to improve mobility in a back that has become stiff through either injury or lack of exercise.

SIDE-SHUNT
This movement can increase flexibility in your lower spine and hips.

1 Relaxed stance
Stand tall, feet hip-width apart and knees soft *(see page 58)*. Relax your arms at your sides and allow your shoulders to drop downwards. Keep your abdominal muscles tensed and maintain a correct pelvic tilt *(see page 66)*.

2 Hip to left
Keeping your upper body as still as possible, and your shoulders in line with your feet, jut your left hip out to the left, transferring your weight onto your left leg and allowing your right knee to bend a little more.

3 Hip to right
Return to your starting position and shunt to the right. Make the sideways movements slow and rhythmical so that you flow from one position to another. Repeat this exercise five times.

KNEE HUGGING WITH RESISTED STRETCH

This exercise is a variation on the simple knee hugging on page 72. The addition of the resisted stretch, in which you push your knees against resistance from your arms, provides extra stretch for the back muscles. **Note**: in this exercise your legs should not move away from your chest during the pushing phase.

1 Knees to chest

Lie on your back, supporting your head on a cushion if you wish. Bend your knees and place your feet on the floor, hip-width apart. Tense your abdominal muscles and gently tilt your pelvis. Bring both knees up towards your chest and grasp them with your hands.

2 Resisted stretch

Now pull your legs slowly towards your chest until you feel a stretch or pulling sensation in the muscles of your lower back. Hold this position and gently but firmly push your knees away from your chest, resisting any movement of your legs with your hands and arms. After three to five seconds, relax and gently pull your knees nearer to your chest again, stopping when you feel any tension or stretching in your lower back. Maintain this new position and repeat the exercise up to a total of three or four times. You should find that this helps to ease any tension in your lower back and that you can bring your knees closer to your chest after each phase of the exercise.

WATCHPOINT

● If grasping your knees hurts, try grasping your lower thighs behind your knees.

EXERCISES

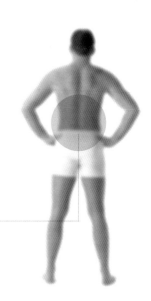

EXTENDED LUMBAR ROLL

This is an extension of the leg-rolling exercise described on page 73 for an acutely painful back. Once you can do that exercise with ease, you can progress to this version to continue to stretch your lower back. As a regular part of a maintenance programme, this exercise should help to improve the flexibility of your lower spine.

1 Starting position

Lie on your back, resting your head on a cushion if you wish. Stretch your arms out to the sides. Keep your shoulders flat and bend your knees, keeping your feet flat on the floor and your knees and feet together. Tilt your pelvis correctly and tense your abdominal muscles.

2 Knees to left

Slowly roll your knees to the left, feeling the stretch spreading up from your hips and into the muscles of your lower back.

3 Knees flat on floor

As your mobility improves, you will probably find that you are able to roll your knees further, eventually touching the floor. Never force this movement. Keep your abddominal muscles tensed, but relax the rest of your body. Breathe slowly and deeply throughout these exercises.

Knees to right 4

Gradually bring your knees back to the starting position, with your feet flat on the floor. Now repeat the sequence in the opposite direction by rolling your knees to the right. Repeat the sequence five times.

EXERCISES

KNEELING PELVIC TILT

This kneeling pelvic tilt stretches the muscles of your lower back. When it is done regularly it can increase flexibility in the lumbar region of your spine. Do not worry if you can only tilt your pelvis a few degrees in both directions. As long as you are aware of a gentle stretch in each direction, you are doing enough to gain some benefit.

1 **Kneeling on floor**

Position yourself on all fours with your knees hip-width apart. Keep your elbow joint 'soft' *(see page 58)* and your hands angled slightly inward. Keeping your neck in line with your back and your chin tucked in, tense your abdominal muscles to support your spine.

2 **Hollow back**

Keeping your abdominal muscles tensed, hollow your spine by tilting the top of your pelvis down towards the floor. Hold for five seconds. Do not force the movement, and stop if it causes any discomfort.

KNEELING STRETCH

When you have completed your repetitions of the kneeling pelvic tilt, relax and stretch out your spine in this position.

1 Back stretching

Kneeling down, sit back on your heels. Tuck your chin down towards your chest and place your hands, palms down, on the floor in front of you, shoulder-width apart. Slowly extend your arms, letting your fingers 'walk' your arms further away. You will feel your back stretching. When you are comfortably stretched, relax your arms and shoulders. Now take deep regular breaths, concentrating on taking in as much air as you can to fill your lungs. Hold for a few seconds and then breathe out, emptying your lungs completely. Feel your ribcage expand and contract as you do this. Relax in this position for a few minutes, concentrating on your breathing. Then sit back on your heels and breathe normally for a minute before getting up.

WATCHPOINTS

● Be careful not to hyperventilate (breathe too rapidly) or you may feel lightheaded.
● If you experience tingling in your hands, relax your arms and bring your elbows back towards your knees so that they are not outstretched.

3 Arched back

Reverse this action by tilting the top of your pelvis upwards. At the same time, tuck in your coccyx (tailbone) and tense your buttock muscles. Your lower back will arch upwards. Keep your abdominal muscles tensed and your neck and jaw relaxed. Breathe slowly and deeply and hold for five seconds. Repeat the sequence five times.

WATCHPOINT

● When arching your back, try to avoid pushing up from your elbows and into your shoulders. Be sure to keep your elbow joints 'soft' all the time.

EXERCISES

SEATED ROTATIONS

The two seated exercises shown here promote rotational mobility of the spine. The exercise using a chair *(see below)* is most suited to those who find sitting on the floor uncomfortable. Start with the seated rotation in a chair and then progress to the variation done sitting on the floor *(right)* when you are able to perform the former with ease.

WATCHPOINTS

● Keep your shoulders relaxed downwards during the exercise.
● Do not turn your head further than shown.
● Breathe normally and keep your jaw relaxed.

SEATED ROTATION IN A CHAIR

Use an upright, firm chair or stool of a height that allows you to sit with your feet flat on the floor and your knees forming a right angle.

Spinal rotation

1 Sit towards the front of a firm, upright chair with your feet firmly on the floor. Tense your abdominal muscles and tilt your pelvis correctly. Lengthen your spine upwards. Reach your right arm down, placing your hand near the back of the chair. Rest your left hand on the outside of your right thigh just above the knee. Slowly rotate your body, pulling your right shoulder back and at the same time pushing your left shoulder forwards. Allow your head and neck to follow (not lead) the movement. Increase the stretch, if it feels comfortable to do so, by exerting gentle pressure on the right thigh with your left hand. Hold the stretch for ten seconds. Slowly return to your starting position and repeat the rotation to the left side. Repeat this exercise five times.

SEATED ROTATION ON THE FLOOR

Try this exercise only when you have mastered the seated rotation in a chair.

1 Stretch to right

Sit on the floor with your left leg straight and your right knee bent. Place your right foot to the outside of your left knee. Tense your abdominal muscles and lengthen your spine. Place your left elbow against the outside of your right thigh and your right hand on the floor behind you. Slowly rotate your body to the right, pushing forwards with your left shoulder and pulling back with your right shoulder. Increase the stretch, if it is comfortable to do so, by pushing your left arm gently against your thigh and turning further to the right. Keep your chin tucked in slightly and do not turn your head any further than shown. Hold for 20 seconds.

Stretch to left

2

Repeat the stretch on the other side. Straighten your right leg. Bend your left knee, placing your left foot on the outside of your right knee. Twist to the left and place your right elbow against the outside of your left leg. Place your left hand on the floor behind you. Now rotate to the left, pushing forward with your right shoulder and pulling back with your left. Hold for 20 seconds. Repeat this sequence five times.

EXERCISES

PRONE STRETCH

This exercise gently stretches your abdominal muscles and at the same time encourages flexibility in your lower back.

1 Upward stretch

Lie on your front, legs together and forehead resting lightly on the floor with your hands, palms down, on the floor, either side of your head. Tuck your elbows in close to your sides. Tilt your pelvis correctly and tense your abdominal muscles. Slowly lever yourself upwards as shown. At the same time stretch your upper body forwards using your arms and shoulders. Only raise your shoulders as far as feels comfortable. Feel your spine lengthen away from your pelvis and stretch your abdominal muscles. Hold this position for five seconds. Slowly lower your shoulders back to the starting position. Repeat the sequence five times.

WATCHPOINTS

● Do not raise your shoulders too high. If your lower back is uncomfortable, increase the pelvic tilt and lower yourself a little. If discomfort or pain persists, discontinue the exercise and hug your knees to your chest (see page 72).
● Remember to breathe normally and remain relaxed throughout the exercise.

EXERCISES

SUPINE STRETCH

This exercise stretches the whole body, from the fingertips to the toes. It provides an excellent all-round stretch and is ideal to finish an exercise session with. From the supine stretch you can conveniently go straight into the relaxation session *(see pages 74–75)*.

1 All-over stretch

Lie on your back with your pelvis tilted correctly *(see page 66)*. Bend your right knee. Stretch your arms out behind your head and imagine that your fingers are being drawn towards the wall behind you. Feel the stretch extending from your fingers to your wrists, elbows and shoulders, and finally allow your whole back to lengthen. At the same time imagine that the toes of your left foot are pulling your left leg away from your body. Feel a stretch extending through the foot, ankle, knee and hip. Breathe deeply and enjoy this all-round stretch. Hold for 20 seconds. Relax and repeat the stretch with your left leg bent and your right leg stretched. You can repeat this exercise if you wish.

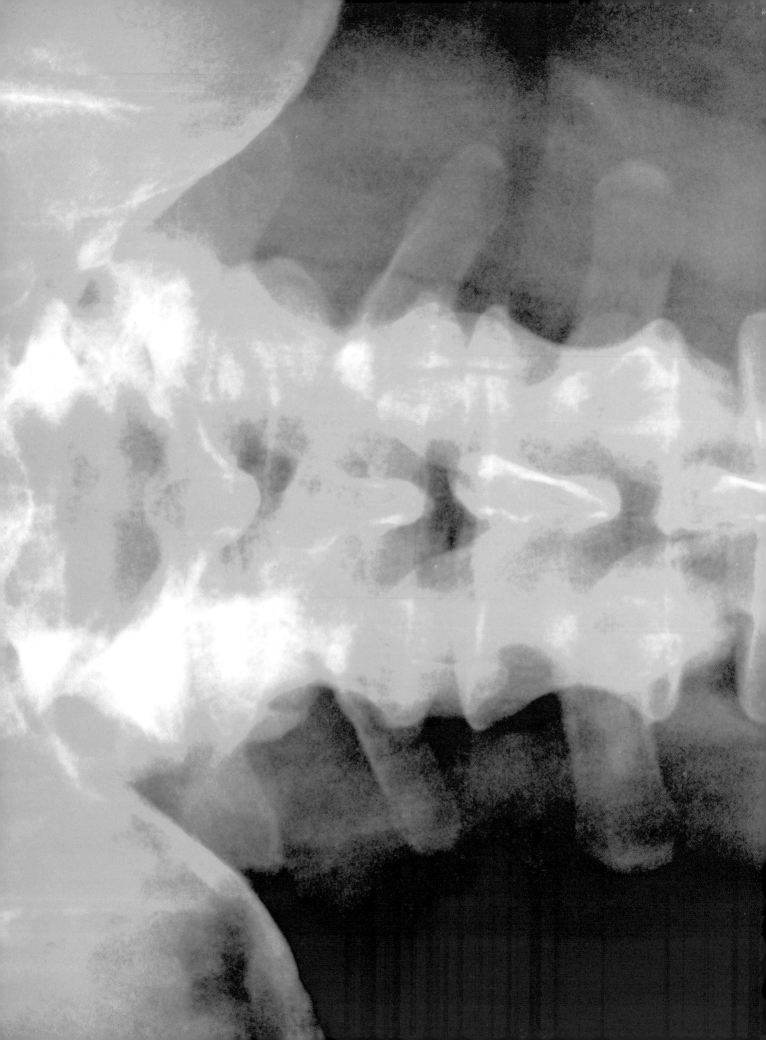

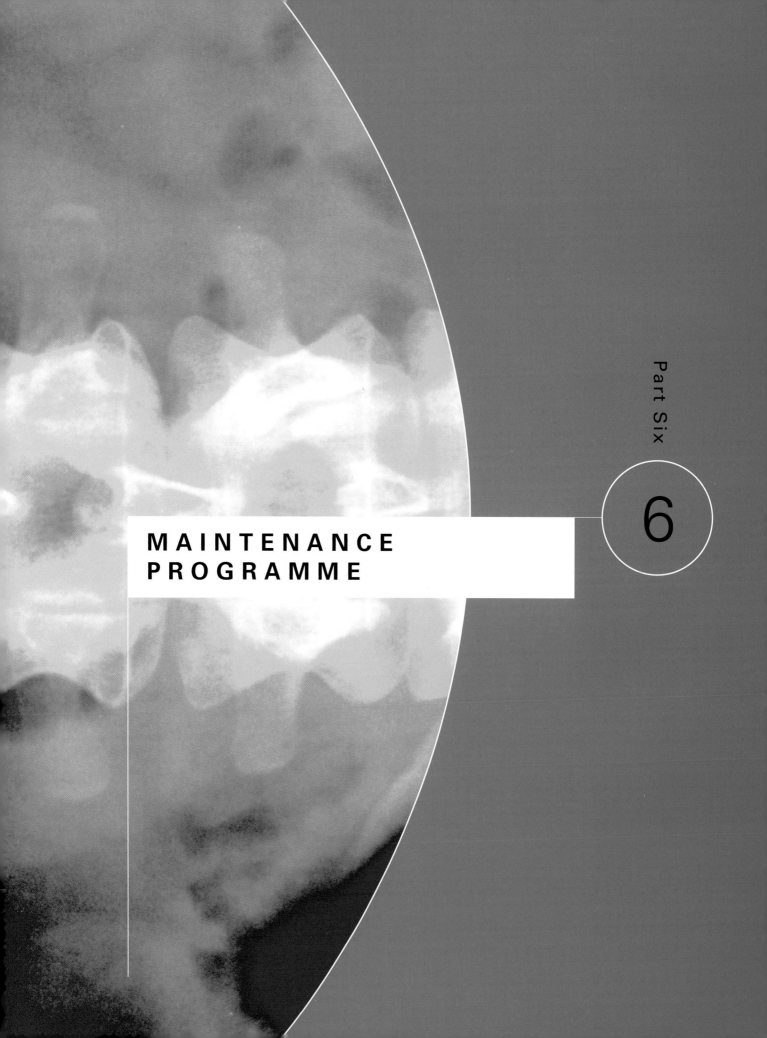

MAINTENANCE PROGRAMME

INTRODUCTION

BACK-MAINTENANCE PROGRAMME

At this stage in your back-care programme you should be free from pain and have made progress in increasing the flexibility of your back through the exercises in Parts Four and Five. Do not embark on these new exercises, particularly the strengthening ones, if you are still finding that the previous exercises cause discomfort. The aim of the maintenance programme is to extend the stretching and flexibility exercises you have already learned. In addition, a variety of strengthening exercises for the back and abdominal muscles is included. These can be quite a challenge for anyone who has a history of back problems or has led a sedentary lifestyle, so approach them with care. It is better to do one correct repetition of an exercise than several incorrect repetitions that may cause strain.

It is important to take into account your own preferences and abilities when you construct your programme. When planning your programme, choose the exercises that you enjoy and that seem most beneficial. If you miss more than a few successive days of a full exercise programme you may need to resume at a less demanding level. Now is also the time to increase your physical activity, taking regular brisk walks and other forms of suitable exercise *(see page 96)*. Always try to maintain a correct posture as this will help to improve the condition of your back *(see page 98)*.

Which exercises, how often and in what order?

The full back-maintenance routine takes longer than that for a recovering back, but it need only be performed once a day. Start with a warm-up, as in the recovering back programme *(see page 80)*. As you feel fitter, you may wish to extend the time given to such exercise.

Although ideally you will do the full maintenance routine once a day, remember to stretch at regular intervals, especially if you have a sedentary job *(see pages 142–147)*.

Having warmed up, you will need to do some stretches. Start with the familiar ones you have already learned *(see pages 80–81)*. Then add the stretches on pages 100–105, along with a quadriceps, a

hamstring and a hip-flexor stretch. Now you are ready to start the strengthening elements. Start with the easiest back and abdominal exercises, the single leg extension *(see page 114)* and the knees-to-chest stomach curl *(see page 122)*. As you become stronger, you will be able to graduate to the more challenging exercises *(see pages 116–119 and 124–129)* and add

some leg lifts *(see pages 130–131)*.
Finish with a selection of stretches
(see pages 132–135), plus any others
you enjoy. Finally, spend some time
relaxing *(see pages 74–75, or the
techniques on pages 136–139)*.

It's your programme

The guidance given on these pages will help you
develop a balanced exercise programme that will
improve the ability of your back to withstand
strain and may reduce the risk of future back
problems. To be effective a programme needs to
be practised regularly and demands commitment.
However, a little regular exercise is better than
no exercise at all, so when you cannot fit in a full
routine, stretch frequently, especially doing the
seated rotation, side and forward stretches.

SAMPLE PROGRAMME

Do exercises from each group (A–E) in the order
shown. Where alternatives are given, start with
the first version and substitute subsequent
exercises as your strength develops. These lists
may seem dauntingly long, but if you are pressed
for time you can choose the exercises you find
most helpful and make up your own sequence.
You will find that some exercises follow on easily
from others and take very little time.

A Warm-up
Two- to five-minute brisk walk.

B Stretch and mobilize
Remember to stretch adequately before and
after the strengthening exercises.

- Pelvic shunt and roll *(see page 101)*
- Upper body stretches *(see pages 102–105)*
- Standing side-bends *(see page 104)*
- Seated rotation *(see page 88)*
- Back warm-ups *(see page 80)*
- Neck rotations and neck side-bends
(see pages 100–101)
- Quadriceps stretch *(see pages 106–107)*

- Hamstring stretch *(see pages 108–109)*
- Hips-to-floor stretch *(see page 110)*
- Pelvic tilts: kneeling *(see page 86)*
- Knee hugging with resisted stretch
(see page 83)
- Extended lumbar roll *(see page 84)* or
extended spinal rotation *(see page 105)*
- Prone stretch *(see page 90)*

C Strengthen the back muscles
Initially do one, then add additional exercises
according to your ability and for variety.
- Single leg extensions *(see page 114)*
- Shoulder lift *(see page 116)*
- Double leg lift *(see page 117)*
- Alternating leg and shoulder lifts *(see page 117)*
- Full back extension *(see page 118)*
- Kneeling stretch and strengthen *(see page 120)*

D Strengthen the abdominal muscles
Start with one exercise from each group below,
then add or exchange another one, according to
your ability and for variety.
- Knees-to-chest stomach curl *(see page 122)* or
advanced abdominal curl *(see page 124)*
- Bridging exercise *(see page 129)*
- Diagonal shoulder lift *(see page 126)* or
diagonal abdominal curl *(see page 127)*
- Arm and leg kneeling stretch *(see page 128)*
- And to strengthen the thigh muscles: leg lifts
(see pages 130–131)

E Cool-down stretches
- Standing curl *(see page 132)*
- Quadriceps stretch *(see page 106)*
- Hamstring stretch *(see pages 108–109)*
- Hips-to-floor stretch *(see page 110)*
- Squatting or sitting stretch *(see pages 133–134)*
- Hurdle sitting *(see page 112)*
- Inner thigh stretch *(see page 113)*
- Supine stretch *(see page 91)*

F Relaxation *(see pages 74–75 and 136–139)*

MAINTENANCE PROGRAMME

IMPROVING OVERALL FITNESS

Once you have recovered from an episode of back pain it is important that you look at the factors in your lifestyle that have contributed to the onset of your back problem. Now, too, is the time to get physically fitter, incorporating the back-maintenance exercises into an increasingly active way of life.

above *People of all ages will benefit from taking more exercise and pursuing a more active lifestyle.*

An active lifestyle

As already discussed, a sedentary lifestyle is one of the main risk factors for back problems. Lack of exercise is also recognized as a major contributory factor to many serious conditions, such as heart disease and osteoporosis. Research has shown that regular exercise can help you to be more alert, give you more energy and may even alleviate some forms of depression.

One of the first things to consider is how to build more healthy physical activity into your daily routine. The type of exercise you choose will depend on your age, interests and fitness level. One of the best forms of exercise for back-pain sufferers is walking. Brisk walking for 20–30 minutes can effectively boost your heart rate and lung function without the risk of back strain that may accompany other forms of exercise, such as golf

or jogging. Try taking a vigorous walk at least three times a week and see how your overall sense of well-being improves. When exercising always wear shoes that have impact-absorbing soles and heels, or fit impact-absorbing insoles. This will help prevent jarring to the joints of your lower limbs and back.

Cycling is another possibility, although initially it can sometimes cause a little neck stiffness and lower backache. Keep your lower back warm while you are cycling, by wearing clothing that does not gape at the waist when you are leaning forward on your bicycle.

Remember that an active lifestyle is not simply a matter of taking exercise. Try to build physical exertion into your everyday activities. For example, take the time to walk or cycle rather than drive, whenever possible, and walk upstairs rather than using an

left It is important to choose a form of exercise that you enjoy, whether this is swimming at your local pool or cycling in the countryside.

below Power-walking offers an excellent way to improve your overall fitness levels.

elevator. Encourage other members of your family, especially children, to take more exercise too, so that they will also reap the benefit of improved health.

Forms of exercise to avoid

Some types of physical activity are not recommended for those with a tendency to back problems. These include sports where the spine is subjected to sudden twisting movements or jarring – for example, squash and high-impact aerobics.

Swimming is often recommended as the ideal exercise for back-pain sufferers. However, unless you are a very competent swimmer and can keep your head low in the water while swimming, breaststroke is best avoided. This is because if your head is out of the water, your back has to arch in order to keep your legs from dipping downwards, thus causing considerable strain on the muscles of your lower back. Backstroke is the ideal stroke to choose because you are lying horizontally on the surface of the water.

Whenever you start a new activity, begin gently and for a short time. If you do not experience any ill effects the next day you can gradually increase the time and

intensity of the exercise. Consult your back-care practitioner if you are unsure if your current or planned sport or activity is suitable for you.

Maintaining a healthy weight

Anyone who is significantly overweight is inevitably increasing the strain on all their weight-bearing joints, including those of the spine. Excess weight is often carried in the abdominal area, and this causes additional strain on the back and affects posture. It is therefore important – for a whole range of medical conditions – to maintain a correct weight *(see page 29)*.

POSTURE CHECKS

One of the key elements in attaining and maintaining a healthy back is learning how to improve your posture. You will be able to take steps to improve your posture as soon as you have recovered from an episode of acute back pain. If you suffer from chronic back pain it is vital that you make improving your posture a priority when planning your back-care programme. Lastly, if you are without back pain at present, by making postural changes and becoming more aware of your body you will be less likely to develop back problems in the future.

Good posture involves using your body in a way that minimizes the strain on any one part of your spine and requires the least amount of muscular effort to maintain. Most people become so used to their habitually poor posture that initially the improved posture feels strange and even uncomfortable. It will therefore require a conscious effort and perseverance to re-educate your muscles and achieve a better, more balanced use of your body.

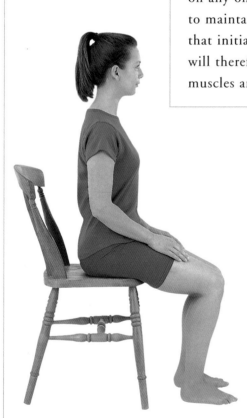

above *Maintaining a good posture when you are sitting minimizes stress in the back.*

Balance: the essence of good posture

The key to good posture is a balanced relationship between the head, neck and back. The muscles of the neck should be relaxed so that the head rests easily on top of the neck and can move freely. When there is tension in the neck muscles, the head is pulled so that it tilts backwards and this creates tension in other areas of the body.

When you are sitting, the force of gravity is transmitted through the spine to the pelvis, and this compresses the lower back. To help relieve this compression, always try to lengthen your neck by imagining that someone is pulling you upwards and very slightly forwards by the hair on the top of your head. As your neck elongates, the rest of your spine will follow, until you are sitting upright with the curves of your spine balanced correctly, as shown left. When sitting like this there is much less strain on your back and it takes very little muscular effort to maintain this position.

Remember to try and relax the rest of your body, letting go of tension, slackening your jaw muscles and allowing your shoulders to drop downwards.

right *Checking and correcting your posture in a mirror is one of the best ways of learning how to stand correctly. See if you can identify any posture faults in this picture.*

Checking your posture

Take time to check and correct your posture throughout the day and always make sure that you check your posture before you start an exercise session.

To begin with it is helpful to check your posture in a full-length mirror. Wearing the minimum of clothing so that you can see your body clearly, and with bare feet, stand sideways on to the mirror and assume your usual posture. Now, starting from your feet, work up your body checking and correcting as you go.

- Both feet should be planted firmly on the floor, hip-width apart.
- Your knees should be very slightly flexed so that the fronts of your knees are above the arches of your feet.
- Your pelvis must be tilted correctly *(see page 66)* and your hips level.
- Lengthen your spine upwards and away from your pelvis towards an imaginary spot on the ceiling just a little in front of you.
- Tense your lower abdominal muscles very gently *(see page 25).*
- Relax your shoulders downwards

so that they are not strained back as if on a parade ground.
- Allow your arms to hang down, completely relaxed, at your sides. Relax your hands and fingers.
- Your head should be balanced on top of your neck, your chin neither tipped downwards nor jutting forward. Your eyes should look forward. Relax your jaw.
- Now check once more that you are lengthening your spine, while remaining relaxed and breathing normally.

You should now be in an almost perfectly balanced standing position. Try closing your eyes and, while maintaining this posture, sway just a few degrees forwards and then backwards. Continue the almost imperceptible swaying until you feel that you are back in balance again in the position that now seems to take the minimum of muscular effort to maintain. This is the balanced sensation that you are seeking to achieve whenever possible throughout the day. Especially try to maintain this sense of balance when you are walking.

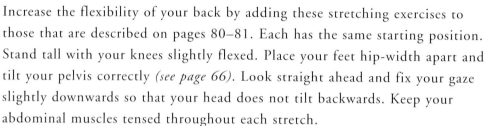

INCREASING FLEXIBILITY

Increase the flexibility of your back by adding these stretching exercises to those that are described on pages 80–81. Each has the same starting position. Stand tall with your knees slightly flexed. Place your feet hip-width apart and tilt your pelvis correctly *(see page 66)*. Look straight ahead and fix your gaze slightly downwards so that your head does not tilt backwards. Keep your abdominal muscles tensed throughout each stretch.

1 Neck rotations

From the starting position, slowly rotate your neck to the left as far as is comfortable, keeping your shoulders still but relaxed. As you breathe out, allow your shoulders to drop further. Hold this position for about five seconds, breathing normally. Slowly return to the starting position. Repeat the rotation to the right. Do a total of five rotations in each direction.

WATCHPOINTS

● Consult your doctor or back-care practitioner before trying these exercises if you have recently suffered from whiplash *(see page 32)* or any other neck injury.

● If you have been suffering from neck pain, complete only one stretch in each direction at first. Slowly increase the repetitions to five if you feel no adverse effects.

● Discontinue if you experience pain during these exercises. If pain occurs some hours later, then omit these exercises.

● Discontinue these exercises if you experience any dizziness, headaches, numbness or any tingling in your fingers.

● Avoid tilting your head backwards while performing these exercises.

2 Neck side-bends

From the starting position, gently tilt your head to the right, moving your ear down towards your shoulder. Take care not to rotate your head or raise your right shoulder. Increase the stretch, if comfortable to do so, by dropping your left shoulder a little further. Breathe normally and hold the stretch for five seconds. Return slowly to the starting position and repeat the tilting movement to the left. Do a total of five stretches in each direction.

3 Pelvic shunt and roll

This exercise is an extension of the basic side-shunt (see page 82). Shunt your pelvis to the left, then roll it forwards, backwards and to the right, in a figure-of-eight pattern. Make the movements slow and rhythmical. Do a total of five figure-of-eight movements.

WATCHPOINTS

● Keep your abdominal muscles tensed throughout the exercise.
● Discontinue the exercise if you experience pain in your back or legs.

STRETCHING THE UPPER BODY

Prepare your upper body for the further exercises in this section by doing this extended programme of stretches. Remember that stretching helps to prevent stiffness that may sometimes follow a strenuous exercise session, as well as increasing your flexibility. The starting position for these exercises is the same: stand tall with 'soft' knees *(see page 58)*, your feet positioned hip-width apart and your pelvis tilted correctly *(see page 66)*. Keep your gaze ahead and slightly downwards. Do not allow your head to tip back.

1 Upward stretch

Interlace your fingers in front of you and then raise your arms above your head, palms facing up. Visualize your arms being pulled upwards. Breathe in slowly and deeply as you push your hands up further. Hold for a few seconds and breathe out as you lower your arms in front of you. Repeat a further four times.

2 Chest stretch

Interlace your fingers behind your back and, as you breathe in slowly and deeply, raise your arms behind your back without leaning forward. Feel the stretch across the front of your chest. As you breathe out, lower your arms slowly. Repeat four more times.

3 Shoulder stretch

Interlace your fingers, palms down, in front of you and then slowly raise your arms until your hands are level with your shoulders. Breathe in slowly and deeply and at the same time push your palms away from you. Feel the stretch in your shoulders and upper back as your lungs fill with air. As you breathe out, slowly lower your arms. Repeat a further four times.

Side-stretch 4

Place your left hand on your left hip and raise your right arm over your head. As you breathe in slowly and deeply, stretch your arm upwards and to the left. As you do so, feel the stretch along your right side from your waist to your upper arm. Be careful not to let your head tilt towards your left shoulder. As you breathe out, slowly lower your arm to the starting position. Repeat the stretch to the left. Do a total of five stretches in each direction.

EXERCISES

EXTENDED SPINAL STRETCHES

These exercises are variations on the side-stretches and leg rolling described on pages 71 and 73 and can help to increase the range of movement in your back. The more you concentrate on controlling your movements, the greater the benefit you will gain from these exercises.

STANDING SIDE-BENDS

It is important not to twist your spine when you are doing this exercise. Keep your hips facing forward.

1 Relaxed stance

Stand tall with your feet hip-width apart. Flex your knees slightly. Relax your arms by your sides and allow your shoulders to drop downwards. Keep your pelvis tilted correctly *(see page 66)* and tense your abdominal muscles.

Bending to left 2

Slowly bend to your left, leading the movement with your shoulder. Allow your left arm to slide down your leg as you bend to the side. Breathe normally, keeping your shoulders relaxed and your spine lengthened. You will feel a stretch in your waist. Only bend as far as is comfortable, then hold this position for five seconds. Slowly return to an upright position. Check your posture *(see step 1)* and repeat, bending to the right. Do five repetitions of this exercise.

WATCHPOINTS

● Do not allow your head to tilt towards your shoulder.
● Do not be concerned if you find you can comfortably bend further on one side than the other. Do not be tempted to overstretch the restricted side.
● Keep your pelvis facing forward throughout the exercise and avoid twisting your spine.

EXTENDED SPINAL ROTATION

This exercise is a variation on leg rolling *(see pages 73 and 84)*. It helps to improve mobility in the lower back and hips and provides a useful stretch for the muscles of the outer thigh.

Legs crossed

1

Lie on your back, supporting your head on a pillow if you wish. Stretch your arms out to the sides and bend your knees. Cross your right leg over the left, keeping your left foot flat on the floor. Tense your abdominal muscles and tilt your pelvis correctly *(see page 66)* so that the hollow of your back is in contact with the floor.

2 ### Legs to left

Keeping your shoulders flat on the floor, gently roll your hips and legs to the left until your left foot reaches the floor. Feel the stretch in your right hip and lower back. Relax and breathe normally for a few seconds. Keeping your right leg crossed over the left, slowly reverse the movement and return to the starting position.

Legs to right

3

Now roll your hips and legs to the right as far as is comfortable, relaxing for a few seconds. You will feel more of a stretch now, as the weight of your right leg exerts downward pressure. Return to the starting position, cross your left leg over your right and repeat. You can do this exercise four more times.

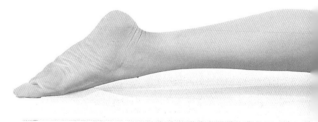

EXERCISES FOR LOWER LIMB MUSCLES

As many of the muscles of the leg attach to the pelvis, lack of flexibility or shortening of these muscles can affect its position and mobility. This in turn can place strain on the lower back and reduce the flexibility of the lumbar spine *(see page 108)*. Proper mobility and function of the lower limb are also essential for minimizing strain on the lower back, especially when lifting and bending. The exercises in this section will help to stretch and improve the flexibility of the muscles of the leg.

QUADRICEPS STRETCHES

The quadriceps femoris (often called the quads) is the large four-part muscle that extends down the front of the thigh from the hip and pelvis to the knee. The main function of this muscle is to extend (straighten) the lower leg, but it is also a flexor muscle of the hip joint. Both the exercises that are shown here provide an effective quadriceps stretch. Choose the one you find most comfortable, or alternate the two to provide variety in your exercise programme.

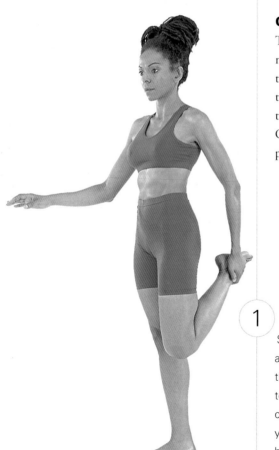

1 Standing quad stretch

Stand tall, steadying yourself against a wall or the back of a chair. Check that your abdominal muscles are tensed and your pelvis is tilted correctly *(see page 66)*. Keeping your right knee 'soft' *(see page 58)*, bend your left knee, bringing your foot up behind you. Clasp your ankle with your left hand and gently ease your foot towards your left buttock. Keep your left knee touching your right knee and your thighs parallel. You will feel a stretch down the front of your left thigh. Hold the stretch for ten seconds. Check your posture and repeat the stretch with your right leg.

1 Lying quad stretch

Lie on your front with your forehead resting comfortably on the back of your left hand. Tense your abdominal muscles and tilt your pelvis correctly. Bring your right foot up towards your right buttock and grasp your ankle with your right hand. Keep your pelvis and your right thigh in contact with the floor. Gently pull your foot down towards your buttock until you feel a stretch in the front of your right thigh. Hold this position for ten seconds and then relax. Repeat the sequence stretching your left leg.

To increase the stretch you can try a resisted stretch. Once you have pulled your foot down towards your buttock, gently push your foot away from you, resisting the push with your hand for five seconds. Then relax your leg and pull your foot down towards your buttock again. You will probably find that your foot will now come closer to your buttock.

WATCHPOINTS

● Try not to arch your back as you pull your leg up behind you. Increasing the pelvic tilt helps to prevent this and adds to the stretch.
● Avoid locking the knee joint of the weight-bearing leg.
● Do not attempt this exercise if you have a painful knee joint.

EXERCISES

HAMSTRING STRETCHES

The hamstrings are the group of muscles at the back of the thigh that extend from the pelvis to the bones of the lower leg (tibia and fibula). Contraction of these muscles extends the hip joint and flexes the knee. The hamstrings are active in walking but relaxed when standing still. Lack of exercise can cause the hamstring muscles to shorten. As the hamstrings attach to the lower part of the pelvis, shortening of the muscle will tilt the pelvis backwards, flattening the normal lumbar curve. This in turn will place additional strain on the muscles of the lower back. Flexible hamstrings are therefore an important factor in the maintenance of low back mobility. Choose whichever of the following hamstring stretches you find most comfortable and convenient. When you are performing these exercises you will also experience a beneficial stretch of the muscles of the calf.

1 Lying hamstring stretch

Lie on your back with your legs bent, your feet flat on the floor and your head resting on a pillow if you wish. Tense your abdominal muscles and tilt your pelvis correctly *(see page 66)*. Raise your right leg and grasp the back of your right thigh with both hands to support your leg. Straighten your leg and raise it as far as you comfortably can. Now flex your foot by pulling your toes towards you. You should feel a strong pulling sensation in the back of your right leg. Hold this position for ten seconds, breathing normally. Repeat a further four times. Repeat the exercise with your left leg for a total of five times.

Note: you are unlikely to be able to raise your leg as far as the model when you first start the exercise programme.

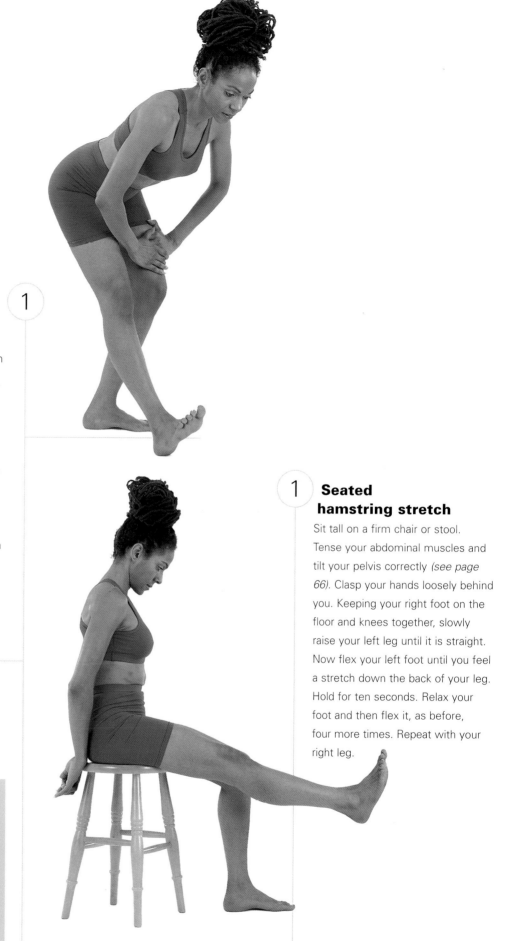

Standing hamstring stretch

Stand upright and bend your left knee, stretching your right leg out in front of you. Lean forward, resting your hands on your left thigh, as shown. Keep your thighs parallel and tense your abdominal muscles. Flex your right foot up towards you until you feel a strong stretch in the back of your right leg. Hold for ten seconds, then relax your foot back down. Repeat this exercise four more times with your right leg, then repeat five times with the left leg.

Seated hamstring stretch

Sit tall on a firm chair or stool. Tense your abdominal muscles and tilt your pelvis correctly *(see page 66)*. Clasp your hands loosely behind you. Keeping your right foot on the floor and knees together, slowly raise your left leg until it is straight. Now flex your left foot until you feel a stretch down the back of your leg. Hold for ten seconds. Relax your foot and then flex it, as before, four more times. Repeat with your right leg.

WATCHPOINTS

● Keep your shoulders, neck and jaw relaxed throughout the exercise.
● To avoid straining your neck while doing this exercise, keep looking down at the flexed foot.

EXERCISES

HIP STRETCHES

These exercises stretch the flexor muscles of the hip, which, when they contract, bring the thigh towards the body *(see page 25)*. These muscles can become shortened in people who spend a lot of time sitting. If practised regularly, these stretches can help to improve your flexibility and your ability to perform a wider variety of exercises more effectively.

HIPS-TO-FLOOR STRETCH

When you first try this exercise you will need to support yourself by holding on to a table or the back of a chair (either in front of you or at your side). If you are already very supple, or as you become so, you may find you are able to rest your hands on the floor to steady yourself, as shown. When you have mastered the first part of this exercise you can increase the stretch.

1   Left leg stretched back

Stand tall, tense your abdominal muscles and tilt your pelvis correctly *(see page 66)*. Place your right foot in front of you, taking your weight on your right leg. Place your left foot a little behind you, resting on your toes. Bend your right knee to lower your body towards the floor. At the same time allow your left leg to slide back behind you so that the left knee is closer to the floor. Keep the right knee positioned directly over the right ankle. You should feel a stretch at the top of your left thigh. Either hold for ten seconds and then return to a standing position and repeat with the other leg, or continue to step 2.

WATCHPOINTS

● To begin with in the hips-to-floor stretch you will probably not be able to lower your pelvis very far towards the floor. As your muscles lengthen, the degree of movement should increase, but do not force it!

● Do not attempt this version of the exercise if you have had hip surgery.

STANDING STRETCH

You may find this variation of the hip stretch easier initially. It is a very simple exercise to do, even at work, and is particularly useful if you have been sitting down for a long time.

Left leg back

1

Stand on your right leg, with your left foot resting comfortably on a surface behind you. This could be the seat of a chair or a table, depending on your height and flexibility. Steady yourself by resting your hand against a wall or chair. Tense your abdominal muscles and tilt your pelvis correctly *(see page 66)* – this is particularly important. Now, without changing the angle of your pelvis or leaning forward, bend your right knee until you feel a stretch in the front of your left hip. Hold for ten seconds and then repeat with your right foot behind you. To increase the stretch, try moving further forward so that your raised leg is straighter.

2 ### Pelvis towards floor

Gently drop your pelvis closer to the floor, taking care not to move your right knee forward of the ankle. Your left leg will slide back further behind you and your knee may touch the ground. It is important not to allow your pelvis to roll to the left. Feel the stretch in the front of your thigh, hip and groin. Hold for ten seconds and return to the starting position. Repeat on the other side.

MORE HIP AND INNER THIGH STRETCHES

Incorporating these gentle stretching exercises for the hips and groin into your back programme will help to ensure that your hip joints are kept as mobile as possible and will also bring some variety to your routine. As with all stretching exercises, start with a very gentle stretch and slowly increase it.

HURDLE SITTING

This exercise stretches the hips and inner thighs, helping to prevent strain in these areas and improve flexibility. It is especially useful for people who sit for long periods, particularly drivers.

1

Right leg back

Sit on the floor with your right leg bent behind you and your left leg bent in front of you, as shown. Move your right knee back as far as you can, so that your thigh is in line with your shoulders. Tense your abdominal muscles and sit as upright as possible, resting your left hand on your left knee and your right hand on your right knee. You should feel a stretching sensation in your hips and inner thigh of your right leg. Hold for 20 seconds. Bring both legs in front of you.

INNER THIGH STRETCH

This is an effective and relaxing exercise for stretching the inner thighs and gently stretching the lower back.

1 Pressure on knees

Sit upright, knees bent out to the sides and the soles of your feet touching. Hold your feet and lean forward a little so that your elbows are resting inside your knees. Very slowly exert a gentle downwards pressure with your elbows to push your knees a little closer to the floor. When you feel a pleasant stretching sensation, maintain – but do not increase – the pressure for 20 seconds, breathing normally and relaxing into the stretch. Keep looking down to avoid straining your neck.

RESISTED INNER THIGH STRETCH

To increase the effectiveness of this stretch, try a resisted stretch variation of the exercise.

1 Resisting pressure

Sit as described in the previous exercise. Now gently try to raise your knees a little, resisting this by holding them in position with pressure from your elbows. Hold for five seconds and then relax your legs. Your knees may now move closer to the floor. Repeat the resisted stretch two more times.

2 Left leg back

Now reverse the position so that your right leg is bent in front of you and your left leg is bent behind. Tense your abdominal muscles and sit as upright as possible, resting your right hand on your right knee and your left hand on your left knee. Hold for 20 seconds.

EXERCISES

BACK STRENGTHENING

The following exercises are designed to strengthen the back muscles. The exercises are graded to become increasingly demanding. Start with the single leg extensions described below and, providing you experience no pain, over a period of weeks you can work progressively through the more challenging exercises on pages 116–119. If you are in any doubt about the suitability of these particular exercises for your back, seek the advice of your doctor or back-care practitioner. After any back-strengthening exercise, always stretch your back muscles by doing the simple knee-hugging exercise *(see page 72).*

SINGLE LEG EXTENSIONS

This exercise strengthens the muscles of the lower back and buttocks. To be effective it has to be done very slowly. Practise it daily for at least a week. If you do not experience any pain, add the shoulder lift *(see page 116)* to your programme.

WATCHPOINTS

● Avoid arching your back.
● Remember to breathe normally as you lift and lower your legs.
● Always lift and lower your legs very slowly, under complete control.
● Keep your jaw relaxed.
● If you experience any back pain stop the exercise, roll onto your back and hug your knees to your chest *(see page 72).*

1 Prone position

Lie on your front with your arms folded so that you can rest your chin or forehead comfortably on them. Tense your abdominal muscles and tilt your pelvis correctly *(see page 66)*.

2 Leg raised

Slowly raise your left leg from the floor, imagining it lengthening away from your hip as it rises. Keeping the leg as straight as possible, feel the muscles in your back and left buttock work to lift your leg. Try to relax your right leg.

3 Leg raising increased

Keep raising your leg as far as you can with comfort, pressing your pelvis to the floor to prevent it from rolling to one side. Hold this position for five seconds and then very slowly lower your leg. Relax and then repeat four more times with your left leg. Repeat the sequence with your right leg a total of five times. As your muscles become stronger, increase the repetitions to ten each side. After you have completed the exercise, hug your knees to your chest *(see page 72)*.

SHOULDER LIFT

This exercise again helps to strengthen the muscles in the back and can improve flexibility of the spine. You will feel your back muscles contracting as they work to lift the weight of your head and shoulders from the floor. Do not attempt shoulder lifts until you have practised single leg extensions *(see page 114)* for at least a week with ease and without pain.

Prone position

1

Lie on your front with your face resting lightly on the ground, feet together and hands resting on your buttocks, as shown. Tense your abdominal muscles and tilt your pelvis correctly *(see page 66)*.

2 ### Shoulders raised

Slowly raise your shoulders from the floor, feeling your back muscles contracting to lift you. As you lift up, imagine your spine lengthening. Fix your gaze on the floor immediately beneath you to prevent tilting your head back. Keep your feet on the floor. When you have lifted your shoulders as high as you comfortably can, hold the position for five seconds and then lower your shoulders slowly back to the floor. Rest for a few seconds and then repeat this exercise, increasing the number of repetitions as your back becomes stronger, to a maximum of ten. When you have completed your repetitions, roll onto your back and hug your knees to your chest *(see page 72)*.

WATCHPOINTS

● Remember to breathe normally, especially when you are holding the lift.
● Keep your jaw relaxed.
● Do not lead the movement with your head; let your shoulders bring your head up. If you tip your head back, you may strain your neck.
● If you experience any back pain, stop the exercise, roll on your back and hug your knees to your chest *(see page 72)*.

DOUBLE LEG LIFT

This exercise may be substituted for the single leg extensions when you have been doing this without discomfort for at least a week.

WATCHPOINTS

● Breathe normally throughout the exercise.
● If you experience pain in your back or legs, discontinue the exercise, roll onto your back and hug your knees to your chest (see page 72).

(1) Both legs raised

Lie on your front with your arms at your sides and your head resting on the floor. Keeping your legs together, tense your abdominal muscles and then those of your buttocks. Moving from the hips, slowly raise your legs a little way from the floor. Keep your legs as straight as possible and your abdominal muscles tense. As you raise your legs, imagine that they are being gently pulled away from your lower back. Hold for five seconds, then lower your legs gradually back to the starting position. As your back muscles become stronger you can repeat the exercise up to a maximum of ten times. When you have completed the exercise, roll onto your back and hug your knees to your chest (see page 72).

ALTERNATING LEG AND SHOULDER LIFTS

After you have been practising the double leg lift comfortably for a few weeks, you can combine the leg and shoulder lift in a single exercise.

(1) Shoulders raised

Start by doing one double leg lift, as above. Relax for a few seconds and then do one shoulder lift. Relax for a few seconds and repeat the sequence. Try to keep the movement rhythmic and smooth for a total of five repetitions. Finish the sequence by rolling onto your back and hugging your knees to your chest (see page 72).

FULL BACK EXTENSION

This is a powerful exercise that strengthens the back and buttock muscles. Build this exercise into your routine when you have been comfortably performing the alternating leg and shoulder lifts *(see page 117)* for at least a week.

1 Prone position

Lie on your front with your forehead resting lightly on the floor. Rest your fingers on your head just behind your ears and hold your elbows out to the sides. Tense your abdominal muscles and tilt your pelvis correctly *(see page 66)*. Keep your legs together.

WATCHPOINTS

● Remember to breathe normally throughout the exercise.

● Lift from your shoulders and not your head, to avoid straining your neck.

● Always lift and lower under complete control.

● Keep your jaw relaxed.

● If you experience any back pain stop the exercise, roll on your back and hug your knees to your chest *(see page 72)*.

2 Shoulders and feet raised

Raise your elbows from the floor to shoulder level, and then slowly lift your shoulders and feet from the floor. As you lift, imagine that your legs are being pulled away from you. Fix your gaze on the floor immediately beneath you to prevent tilting your head back.

Position held

Continue to rise as far as you can with comfort. Hold for three to five seconds and then slowly lower your shoulders and legs to the floor, using your back muscles to control the movement. Repeat this sequence

3

four more times, gradually increasing the number of repetitions to ten as your back becomes stronger. After completing the exercise, roll onto your back and hug your knees to your chest *(see page 72).*

KNEELING STRETCH AND STRENGTHEN

This exercise combines an effective stretch for the back with a movement that strengthens the extensor muscles of the back and the gluteal muscles in the buttocks. Throughout this exercise your pelvis should remain horizontal, so make sure you do not allow it to roll to one side, especially in steps 3 and 4.

1 Kneel on floor

Position yourself on all fours with your knees hip-width apart. Keep your elbows 'soft' *(see page 58)* and your hands angled inward slightly. Tuck in your chin slightly to prevent neck strain and keep your gaze fixed between your hands.

WATCHPOINTS

● Keep your abdominal muscles tensed at all times.
● Do not tilt your head upwards as you raise your leg behind you. Keep looking at the floor, with your chin tucked in.
● Breathe normally throughout the exercise.

2 **Knee towards chin**

Tense your abdominal muscles and gradually bring your left knee up towards your chin until you feel a gentle stretch in your lower back. Hold for five seconds, while breathing normally.

Knee back

Keeping your abdominal muscles tensed, slowly extend your left leg backwards, keeping your knee bent as you do so.

3

4 **Leg raised**

Continue to push back and raise your leg, concentrating on lifting your thigh until it is horizontal, as shown. Do not let your pelvis tip or roll as you raise your leg. Imagine that your leg is being gently pulled away from you. Hold this position for five seconds. You will feel your abdominal, lower back and buttock muscles working hard to support your leg and keep your pelvis stable. If you feel any discomfort, check you are doing this exercise correctly and stop if the discomfort continues. Repeat the exercise four more times with your left leg and then do five repetitions with your right leg.

EXERCISES

ABDOMINAL CURLS

Stomach curls are simple and effective strengthening exercises for the abdominal muscles. Start with the knees-to-chest version *(see below)* and after a few weeks, when your muscles are stronger, progress to the advanced abdominal curl *(see page 124)*. Do not do both exercises in the same session.

KNEES-TO-CHEST STOMACH CURL

As well as strengthening your abdominal muscles, this exercise stretches your lower back.

1 Legs curled

Lie on your back with your head on a small cushion if you wish. Place your feet flat on the floor and keep your knees together. Either rest your hands on the floor beside you with your palms facing down, or above your head (as shown here), whichever is more comfortable for you. Tense your abdominal muscles. Breathe out while bringing your knees towards your chest.

2 Knees towards chin

By contracting your abdominal muscles, tip your pelvis towards your chest so that your knees are brought nearer to your chin. Hold this position for a few seconds, breathing normally, before returning slowly to the starting position, breathing in as you do so. Repeat four more times.

Knees to chest 3

As your abdominal muscles become stronger you may find that you are able to bring your knees closer to your chest. When you do so you will find it easier to raise your feet a little as you curl, as shown. Gradually increase the number of repetitions that you do to a maximum of ten.

WATCHPOINTS

● Pay particular attention to your breathing when you do this exercise. Breathe out as you bring your knees towards you and breathe in as you relax.
● Keep your neck and jaw relaxed.
● Do not hurry. The slower and more controlled the exercise, the more effective it is.
● If you find that this exercise causes pain, check that you are doing it correctly and, if discomfort persists, omit it from your exercise programme.

ADVANCED ABDOMINAL CURL

This is a powerful strengthening exercise for the abdominal muscles. It should be attempted only after you have spent a few weeks practising the knees-to-chest stomach curl *(see page 122)*. Do not expect to find this exercise easy at first. With regular practice, however, you will notice the strength in your abdominal muscles increasing and you will be able to curl further and increase the number of repetitions.

1 Ankles crossed and legs curled

Lie on your back on the floor, knees together and drawn up towards your chest with your ankles crossed. Rest your arms out at shoulder level and place your fingertips behind your ears, as shown.

WATCHPOINTS

● Lead the movement with your shoulders, not your elbows or head.

● Breathe out as you contract your abdominal muscles and curl up. Breathe in as you return to the starting position.

● Do not strain your neck muscles or clench your jaw. If you experience discomfort in your neck, check that you are not pulling on your head with your fingers (they should only be resting on, and not holding, your head). If neck discomfort persists, revert to the knees-to-chest stomach curl *(see page 122)*.

● If you find that the exercise is causing you back pain, check that you are doing it correctly and, if discomfort persists, discontinue the exercise.

2 Shoulders raised and knees curled

As you breathe out, tense your abdominal muscles, raise your shoulders and curl your pelvis up from the floor. Bring your shoulders and knees towards each other as far as you can without strain. Hold for a few seconds, breathing normally, then slowly return to the starting position, breathing in as you do so. Repeat four more times.

3 Increasing the curl

As your muscles become stronger you may be able to bring your shoulders and knees closer together, and you may gradually increase the repetitions to a maximum of ten.

STRENGTHENING THE OBLIQUE ABDOMINAL MUSCLES

The oblique abdominal muscles help to give support to the spine in twisting movements of the trunk. Practise the diagonal shoulder lift for a few weeks, before progressing to the more challenging diagonal abdominal curl. Do not do both exercises in the same session.

DIAGONAL SHOULDER LIFT

To perform this shoulder lift correctly, you should lead the exercise with your shoulder, and not with either your elbows or your head.

1 Legs bent

Lie on your back with both knees bent and your feet flat on the floor. Stretch your right arm out to the side at shoulder level. Place the fingertips of your left hand behind your ear and rest the bent arm on the floor. Tilt your pelvis correctly *(see page 66)* and tense your abdominal muscles. Breathe in.

2 Left shoulder to right hip

Now raise your left shoulder from the floor towards your right hip, breathing out as you do so. Allow your head and neck to follow the movement. When you have raised your shoulder as far as is comfortable (this may not be very far to begin with), slowly lower yourself back to the starting position, breathing in as you do so. Repeat four more times with your left shoulder and then repeat the exercise moving your right shoulder towards your left hip five times.

DIAGONAL ABDOMINAL CURL

After you have practised the diagonal shoulder lift for a few weeks and you are able to do it with ease, then you can substitute this more demanding exercise.

Shoulders to knees

Lie on your back on the floor, knees together and drawn up towards your chest with your ankles crossed. Rest your fingertips behind your ears and hold your elbows out at shoulder level. Breathing in, now raise your shoulders from the floor towards your knees, as far as you can with ease.

Left shoulder to right knee

As you breathe out, bring your left shoulder towards your right knee as far as is comfortable. Hold for a few seconds, breathing normally, and then breathe in slowly as you return to the starting position. Repeat the sequence bringing your right shoulder towards your left knee. Do a total of five curls in each direction, alternating left and right. As your muscles become stronger, you will be able to pull your shoulders and knees closer together and you may gradually increase the repetitions to a maximum of ten in each direction.

LOWER BACK STABILITY EXERCISES

These two exercises strengthen the abdominal and back muscles to help stabilize and protect the lower back. The kneeling exercise given below should only be attempted once you have practised and are comfortable with the kneeling exercise described on pages 120–121.

OPPOSITE ARM AND LEG KNEELING STRETCH

Do this sequence twice to start with, gradually working up to five repetitions on each side of the body.

(1) **Left leg straightened**

Position yourself on all fours, making sure that your knees are directly under your hips and your hands are under your shoulders. Fix your gaze on the floor just in front of your hands and keep your neck in line with your spine. Tense your abdominal muscles and slowly extend and then raise your left leg until it is level with your hip. Imagine it being drawn out behind you as you lift. Concentrate on keeping your pelvis in the starting position; do not let it rotate or tip forward or back.

(2) **Left leg and right arm outstretched**

Keeping your abdominal muscles tensed, slowly lift your right arm until it is level with your shoulder. Gently stretch it away from your shoulder and hold this position for a few seconds, before slowly lowering your arm and leg and returning to the starting position. Repeat the exercise, lifting your right leg and your left arm.

WATCHPOINTS

● Do not let your back arch.
● Keep your neck lengthened throughout the exercise.
● Breathe normally throughout.

BRIDGING EXERCISE

Before starting this exercise, look carefully at step 2 so that you know the position you need to achieve. It is also important that you raise and lower yourself very slowly to obtain maximum benefit from the exercise.

1 Knees bent

Lie on your back with your head and shoulders supported on a pillow if you wish. Bend your knees and place your feet flat on the floor. Rest your arms at your sides or fold then over your chest.

2 Pelvis raised

Raise your pelvis from the floor, contracting your buttock muscles as well as your abdominal muscles as you lift. Ensure that your back does not arch upwards. Imagine a straight line passing from your knees, through your pelvis and abdomen, to your upper back. Make sure that your weight is taken by your upper back and shoulders to reduce strain on your neck. Hold this position for ten seconds, contracting your abdominal muscles firmly. Now slowly lower yourself back to the starting position. Repeat four more times. As you become stronger, you can try extending one leg when you are in the bridging position, holding it outstretched for several seconds.

LEG LIFTS

This exercise is useful as it strengthens the muscles of the buttocks and thighs. The more slowly you raise and lower your leg, the more beneficial the exercise will be to you. If you find that your neck feels uncomfortable when it is propped on your hand as shown, then you can use a pillow on the floor to support your head.

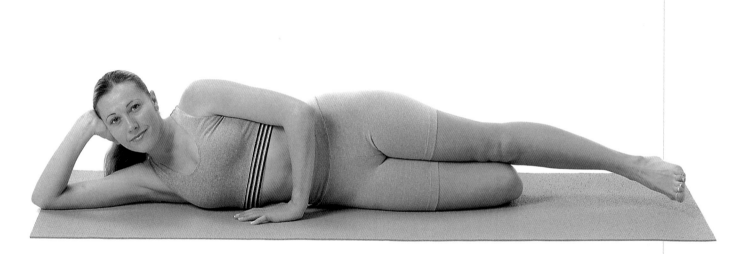

1 Lying on side, right leg bent

Lie on your right side so that your hips are vertical. Rest on your right elbow with your head supported in your hand. Bend your right leg, bringing your knee slightly in front of you to help you balance. Keep your left leg straight and in line with your body. For increased stability, put your left hand on the floor in front of you.

WATCHPOINTS

● Keep your straightened leg in line with your body.
● Make sure that your hips remain vertical and that they do not roll.

2 Left leg raised

Tense your abdominal muscles and buttocks. Breathe in slowly as you raise your left leg as far as is comfortable. Keep your foot flexed towards the shin throughout the exercise. Visualize your leg lengthening away from the hip. Do not allow your pelvis to roll forward or backward. Hold your leg in this position for five seconds before lowering it as you breathe out. Repeat four more times.

Left leg bent   3

Remaining on your side, straighten your right leg. Bend your left leg and rest your left knee on the floor in front of you.

4 Right leg raised

Tense your abdominal muscles and, keeping your right foot flexed towards your shin, breathe in as you raise your right leg so that the foot rises from the floor. Hold for five seconds and then breathe out as you lower the leg. Repeat four more times. Turn onto your left side and repeat the entire sequence, first raising your right leg, as in step 2, and then your left leg, as in step 4.

MORE SPINAL STRETCHES

As you exercise more to increase the strength of your back muscles, it is important to balance this activity with a wide variety of stretching exercises to maintain flexibility and prevent stiffness. Choose a selection of cool-down spinal stretches to do after you have completed the back-strengthening part of your programme. You may like to include some from pages 104–105.

STANDING CURL

This exercise acts as a good stretch for the whole of the spine. Do not, however, try to touch your toes.

Back curling over

1 Stand tall with your feet hip-width apart, pelvis tilted correctly *(see page 66)* and abdominal muscles tensed. Bend your knees a little and allow your arms to hang relaxed at your sides. Tuck your chin into your chest and slowly bend your neck forwards, starting at the base of your skull. Working downwards, continue to curl the rest of your spine forwards and downwards until the curl reaches your pelvis. Stretch your arms downwards to gently increase the stretch across your shoulders. Hold the position for ten seconds, breathing deeply and evenly. Now place your hands on your thighs for support and slowly uncurl upwards from the lower back.

WATCHPOINTS

● Keep your knees bent and your abdominal muscles tensed throughout the exercise.
● Breathe normally as you curl and uncurl.
● Never force the curl by trying to touch your toes.

SQUATTING

This position provides an effective stretch for the lower back and the muscles of your legs. It is a particularly good exercise if your lower back is feeling stiff and aching after spending a long time standing still or walking slowly, for example during a prolonged shopping trip. It can be done anywhere – you can always squat down and pretend to tie your shoelaces or pick something up from the floor! For some people, this exercise is much harder than it looks and many people find it difficult to balance when they first try squatting. If this applies to you, try squatting with your back close to a wall for support, or have a piece of heavy furniture close by to hold on to.

1 Squat to floor

Tense your abdominal muscles and, with your feet wide apart and pointing slightly outwards, lower yourself into a squatting position, keeping your abdominal muscles tensed. Do not worry if you are not able to go down very far initially, as this should improve with practice. Hold on to something to give you support, or rest your hands on the floor, as shown. Keep your arms between your knees and your knees over your toes. When you are comfortable, increase the stretch by tucking your chin into your chest. Hold for 20 seconds and then stand up, using your leg muscles and keeping your back as straight as possible. Breathe normally throughout the exercise.

WATCHPOINTS

● Do not do this exercise if you experience pain or discomfort in the knees.
● Do not bounce while you are squatting.
● Keep your chin tucked down as you stand, to avoid straining your neck.

SITTING STRETCH

This gentle back-stretching exercise is both simple and effective. It is a very comfortable and calming position and may be used for brief relaxation when it is not possible or appropriate to lie down.

1 Body curled

Sit on the floor with your knees bent and your feet flat on the floor. Slowly curl forward, so that your head is resting on or just between your knees. Close your eyes and relax your jaw. Allow your arms to stretch down along your shins. Feel your back stretching and your shoulder blades opening as you stretch your hands towards your feet. Try not to raise your shoulders towards your ears, but let them relax outwards and downwards on either side of your knees. Breathe in and out slowly and deeply, concentrating on expanding your ribcage as you breathe in. Hold the stretch for at least 30 seconds, or longer if you wish.

SEATED FORWARD STRETCH

This is a gentle stretching exercise for the back and hamstring muscles. It is good to do this after performing the strengthening exercises and as part of a cool-down stretching routine. To balance the hamstring stretch, you can add a quadriceps stretch from pages 106–107.

1 **Hands towards ankles**

Sit on the floor with your legs straight out in front of you. Stretch your arms out, with your hands resting on your legs, as shown. Tense your abdominal muscles and slowly curl downwards, starting from the top of your spine and working down to the base until you feel a pleasant stretch in your back and legs. Allow your arms to slide down your legs towards your ankles so that you can feel your shoulder blades stretching too. To avoid straining your neck, keep your chin towards your chest and look at your toes. Relax into the stretch, remembering to breathe slowly and deeply. Hold the stretch for 20 seconds and then slowly uncurl. As you become more flexible you will find that you will be able to stretch further and further down towards your feet. You may also like to hold the position for longer. You can increase the hamstring and calf stretch in this exercise by flexing your feet towards your shins.

WATCHPOINT

● If you find it too uncomfortable to sit with your legs straightened, then allow them to bend a little at the knee. A small cushion placed under your knees might feel more comfortable. It is especially important to do the hamstring stretches on pages 108–109.

● Do not attempt to bounce towards your toes.

RELAXATION

The value of relaxation cannot be underestimated, both in resolving and preventing back problems. Suffering from back pain can be physically and emotionally draining, as sleep is often disturbed and unrefreshing. This makes coping with everyday tasks more difficult. It is also not unusual to feel a little dispirited if back pain persists for more than a few days, as the possible implications of a bad back on your future lifestyle become a concern. It is at times like these that a regular session of relaxation can help your recovery.

Once you have learnt effective relaxation techniques, they are always a useful tool to help overcome the stresses of our increasingly frenetic lives. Therefore, take time to learn how to relax. It is a skill that does not come easily to most people and will require a little effort and perseverance on your part, but once mastered it is invaluable.

Setting the scene

Ideally you should always try and allow for a period of relaxation, however brief, after an exercise session. The relaxation technique described on pages 74–75 is ideal for this purpose and follows on conveniently from the supine stretch (see page 91). This particular technique is also excellent if you are in acute pain, and can be used for brief but frequent periods of relaxation while you are resting in bed.

However, for deeper relaxation that will have a greater calming effect, enabling you to free yourself of the accumulated stresses and strains of everyday life, especially if you are experiencing back pain, there are other relaxation techniques that you may wish to try. For the relaxation to be effective you will need to set aside approximately 20–30 minutes, preferably every day, until you have mastered the technique; once you have done so, 10–15 minutes daily may well be sufficient time.

Choose a period of the day when it is convenient for you to devote sufficient time for relaxation without the pressure or demands of

below *Transport yourself in your imagination to a warm and safe place where you can relax completely, away from the stresses of the world.*

other tasks to distract you. You will not want to be disturbed, so make sure that everyone in the house knows that you are relaxing and unplug the telephone.

Wear comfortable, loose-fitting clothing and choose a room that is warm but well ventilated. You may wish to play some soothing background music, but avoid anything with an obvious beat or with words. It can be helpful to have an object in the room to focus on; popular items include a lighted candle, a flower or even a glass of water.

The position that you choose for relaxation is a matter of personal preference, but the most popular position is sitting in a chair, preferably a firm one with a supportive back.

Sit up tall *(see page 98)*, with both feet on the floor and your hands resting, palm upwards, on your thighs. Beware of lying down in bed to relax, as you will probably go to sleep! Sleeping after you have completed your relaxation session is fine, but try to stay awake while you are actually relaxing in order to gain the maximum benefit from the session.

Now try the different relaxation techniques that are described on the following pages.

below *Focusing on the flickering flame of a candle can help to clear the mind of distractions and aid relaxation.*

1 Either close your eyes or focus on one particular object, for example a flickering candle flame or a flower.

2 Become aware of your breathing (see pages 60–61). Begin to breathe slowly and deeply, in through your nose and out through your mouth. As you breathe in, imagine that you are gathering tension from all the different parts of your body, starting from your hands and feet, and sucking that tension into your lungs. Now, as you breathe out, imagine that you are deliberately expelling these tensions from your lungs, out into the atmosphere where they dissipate and cannot harm you. With each breath you will find that you have fewer tensions to collect and expel, until you are feeling completely relaxed.

3 Continue to concentrate on your breathing for 20 minutes or so, keeping your body completely relaxed. If any anxieties or worries come into your mind, make a mental note to deal with them later and then breathe them out, together with any tensions in your body that might have become apparent.

4 When it is time to finish your relaxation session, open your eyes or change your focus to look at another object. Allow yourself a few more moments of quiet before stretching your limbs and then slowly getting up. Do not rush, but allow yourself a little time before getting back to your usual activities.

An alternative to concentrating solely on your breathing is to use your imagination to transport yourself into a relaxing situation. You could recall a pleasant memory, such as a summer holiday. Recall the sensations of lying on the beach, with the sun's warmth enveloping your body while you gaze at the fringe of the parasol moving gently in the wind. All is quiet except for the sound of the waves lapping on the shore. You have nothing to do but relax.

Alternatively, build up in your imagination a picture of your ideal relaxation environment. This might be lying in long grass on a hillside watching the seed-heads of the grasses sway in the breeze, which caresses and cools you while a skylark sings high in the sky. Or you could be lying on an inflatable mattress in a swimming pool watching the leaves of a nearby tree shimmer in the heat; you are slowly rocking and bobbing on the water, which is gently lapping against the sides of the pool.

Your ideal location could be absolutely anywhere, just as long as it is warm, quiet and comfortable, and you feel safe and secure. Remember to breathe slowly and deeply, to relax your muscles, especially your jaw, empty your mind and let your imagination carry you away!

Sometimes it is helpful to repeat a single word over and over in your mind in rhythm with your breathing as you visualize. For example, a word like 'warm' is a pleasant way to feel and can be repeated slowly with a long, drawn-out syllable: 'warrrrrrrrrrrrrrrrrrrm'.

As with any skill, once you have learned how to relax you will find that it becomes easier to enter into a relaxed state. To reap the full benefits of relaxation you should try and set aside a specific time every day when you can relax. Initially you will need to allow about half an hour but, as you become more skilled at relaxation techniques, you will find that as little as ten minutes will be of benefit. Therefore try to plan a particular time for relaxing in your daily routine. You will find that you feel calmer, yet have more energy and are better able to cope with stress as a result, benefiting both your mental and your physical health.

Learn to recognize the signs of stress and take preventative action to stop these building up by taking a relaxation break.

Among the most common symptoms of stress are rapid, shallow breathing, breath-holding or sighing. A tense jaw and clenched teeth, or constant tapping with the foot or fingers, are also telltale signs of stress. If prolonged, stress can cause irritability, frequent headaches and a poor sleep pattern – either difficulty in getting to sleep or waking early in the morning. You may find that at times you experience one or more of these symptoms. You now have a tool to help alleviate them and make a positive contribution to your overall physical and emotional well-being.

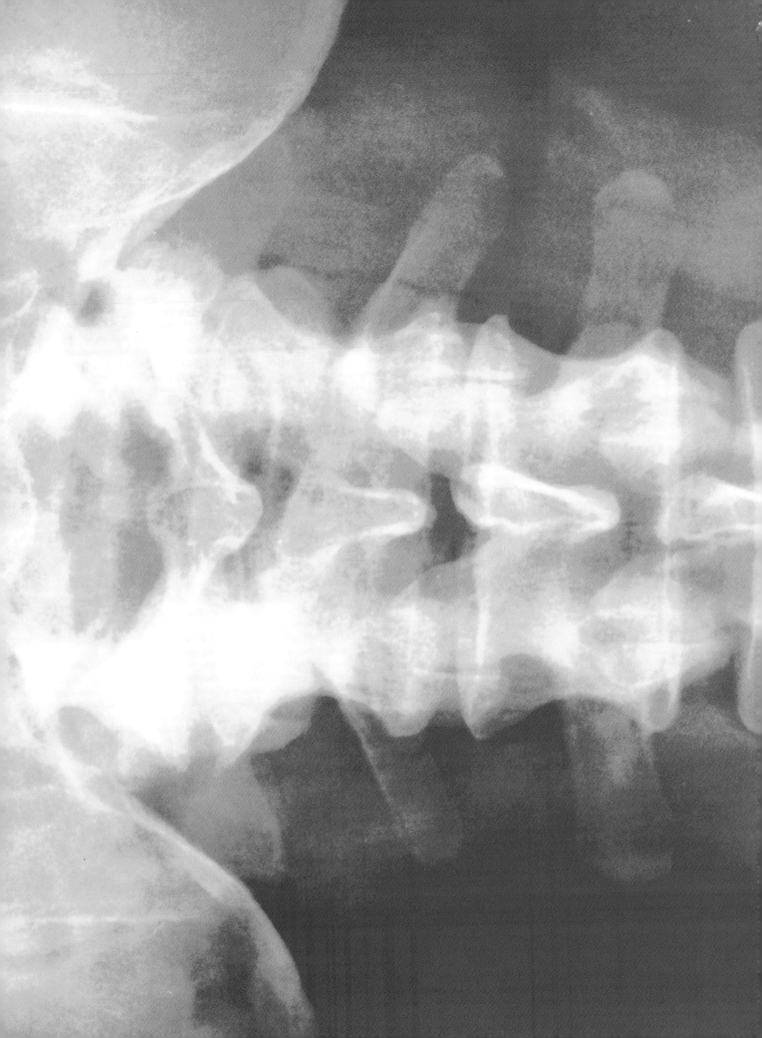

EXERCISES FOR
THE WORKING DAY

INTRODUCTION

WORKING POSTURE

Two of the most common causes of chronic back trouble are poor posture and too much time spent sitting down – both of which place additional stresses on the spine and its supporting structures. If you spend your working day sitting at a desk or in a car you are at particular risk from back trouble. Therefore you should pay special attention to your posture and ensure that the relative height of your desk and chair are correct (or in the case of a car, seat and steering wheel). It is also vital to give yourself regular breaks throughout the working day, either from your desk or vehicle, so that you can stretch your back. This is particularly important if you already suffer from a back problem.

The exercises that are described on the following pages can be performed easily in an office or other place of work. Don't be embarrassed about doing them. Once you start these exercises, you will probably be surprised by how many of your colleagues will admit to having back problems themselves and will want to find out more about your approach to back care. If you have any difficulty in adjusting your office furniture to the correct height you should discuss this with your employer.

There are now some excellent, ergonomically designed office chairs. However, even the best chair is of little help if it is not adjusted correctly. Here are some pointers on how to adjust your chair:

1 Raise the seat so that your hips are slightly higher than your knees when you are sitting with both feet flat on the floor. Your pelvis should now be in a balanced position, neither tipping backwards nor forwards. Ideally, your chair seat should tip forward slightly to reduce the pressure on the back of your thighs.

2 Adjust the back of the chair so that, when you are sitting upright, your back is fully supported. If you have an adjustable lumbar support, make sure that it is inflated to fit snugly and comfortably into your lumbar curve. If there is no built-in lumbar support, then a small cushion or a towel folded into a pad may be helpful.

An ideal chair is one that pivots and moves with you as you lean backwards and forwards so that your spine remains continually in

Using the telephone

● Do not cradle the handset between your ear and shoulder.
● Use a headset if you are on the telephone for a significant part of the working day.

contact with the back of the chair and is supported at all times.

When you are sitting, try not to slump in your chair, as this tends to compress your lungs and abdomen, restricting your breathing and impairing your digestion and the circulation in your legs. To avoid this, always remember to lengthen your spine, drawing yourself upwards to a balanced, poised and comfortable position.

If you are using a computer for much of the day, the top of the monitor should be just above eye level when you are sitting correctly. Make sure that both the monitor and the keyboard are directly in front of you, so that you are not twisting by even a few degrees. Your forearms should be level when your fingers are resting on the middle row of letters on the keyboard, ideally with your wrists on a wrist support.

If you spend a considerable amount of time on the telephone consider using a headset. Beware of supporting the handset on your shoulder by raising your shoulder and tilting your head, as this will cause tension in your neck and upper back. If you follow these guidelines you are less likely to suffer from back complaints due to sitting at work.

Sitting position

● Head in a vertical line with the shoulders and buttocks.
● Hips slightly higher than knees.
● Feet hip-width apart.
● Back of chair adjusted to support the spine.

Desk height and computer position

● For typing, align your elbow with the middle row of the keyboard.
● For writing, have your elbow a little below desktop height.
● For computer work, the top of the screen should be level with your eyes when looking straight ahead.

DESK STRETCHES

If you work at a desk for much of the day, make sure that you give your body a break at least every hour or so by getting up and doing the circulation booster sequence *(see below)*. In addition, try to do a selection of the stretches on the following pages at least three times during the working day, aiming to do each exercise at least once a day. Perform the exercises that you find most helpful more frequently. Remember that the same cautions apply to these exercises as to those that you do at home: do not force a stretch beyond the point of comfort, stop if you experience any pain and breathe normally.

1 Shoulder stretch

Push your chair back from your desk. Interlace your fingers, palms down in front of you, and raise your arms until your hands are level with your shoulders. Breathe in slowly and deeply and at the same time push your palms away from you. Feel the stretch in your shoulders and upper back as your lungs fill with air. As you breathe out, slowly lower your arms. Repeat a further four times and then do the same exercise with your hands raised above your head.

Circulation booster

When you stand up from your desk, take several deep breaths and then walk around for a few minutes. As you do so, shake your arms at your sides to loosen your fingers, wrists, elbows and shoulders. Then slowly rise up onto your toes and equally slowly lower your heels to the floor again. Repeat this five times before sitting down again or continuing with some stretches.

2 Side-stretch

Sit tall with your pelvis tilted correctly *(see page 66)*. Tighten your abdominal muscles. Link your hands and raise them above your head. Bend slowly a few degrees to your right until you feel a stretch down your left side. Hold for a few seconds, then return to the centre. Now bend to the left. Do a total of five bends in each direction.

3 Forward stretch

Sit towards the front of your chair with your legs slightly apart. Sit tall and tense your abdominal muscles. Keeping them tensed, tuck your chin to your chest and slowly curl forward, imagining your spine slowly stretching and opening, starting at your neck and working down to your lower back. This movement should take you at least ten seconds. Allow your arms to stretch down between your knees. Try not to rock forward through your hip joints and keep your pelvis tilted correctly *(see page 66)*. Breathe normally, relax and enjoy the stretch for 10–20 seconds.

4 Seated rotations

Sit upright on your chair. Turn to grasp the left side of the chair back with your right hand. Rest your left hand on the back of the chair. Gently rotate your body further to the left by pulling with your right hand against the chair back. Keep your pelvis facing forward. Hold the stretch for ten seconds, then reverse your hand positions and rotate to the right. Repeat twice.

5 Pelvic rocking

This exercise can be done unobtrusively at your desk at any time. Sit tall with your shoulders relaxed. Tip your pelvis forward so that your back arches. Then tense your abdominal muscles and tilt your pelvis in the opposite direction. Repeat these rocking movements a further five times.

6 Seated knee hug

Sit tall with your feet on the floor and knees hip-width apart and tilt your pelvis correctly *(see page 66)*. Tense your abdominal muscles and raise your right knee. Grasp your raised leg around the shin and pull it gently towards your chest. Hold for ten seconds. Repeat with the left leg, then repeat the sequence twice more.

WALL-SUPPORT SHUNT

This is an easy exercise to stretch your waist, hips and lower back, which you can perform away from your desk against any convenient wall.

(1) Arm against wall

Rest your left forearm against a wall at shoulder height. Now move your legs further away from the wall so that you are leaning against the wall supported by your arm. Stand tall, tense your abdominal muscles and tilt your pelvis correctly *(see page 66)*.

Hip towards wall (2)

Without moving your feet, move your left hip in towards the wall so that your body is vertical and your legs are leaning in further, as shown. Hold for ten seconds and repeat twice more. Turn around and repeat the exercise a total of three times, leaning on your right arm.

THE BASICS OF EVERYDAY BACK CARE

During the day try to be conscious of your posture, correcting it accordingly *(see pages 98–99)*. If your work is sedentary, follow the advice on pages 142–147; if you have to drive for long periods, see pages 150–153. Attention to the following points may help you avoid back problems.

above *Whenever possible, split one heavy load into two lighter parts so that you can balance the weight.*

- The fundamental points of achieving a better posture are simple. Just remember to tilt your pelvis correctly *(see page 66)* and tense your abdominal muscles very slightly. Lengthen your neck and spine upwards, while relaxing your shoulders downwards. This can be done both while standing and sitting.

- Sit in chairs that provide good support for your spine and try to avoid slumping, especially when relaxing – for example, when watching television. If a chair does not provide adequate support, place a small cushion in the lumbar area of your back. Whenever possible, avoid sitting for more than an hour without getting up and walking around, however briefly. Do a few of the stretching exercises when you can.

- If you suffer from persistent or recurrent backache, especially if it is associated with stiffness in the morning, consider changing your bed. A bed that is good for the back should be neither too hard nor too soft, providing adequate support for your spinal curves when you lie on your back and side. Contrary to popular belief, a very firm, orthopaedic-type bed is not usually the bed of choice for most back-pain sufferers. If your partner is very different in weight, then consider two separate single mattresses zipped together.

- Avoid standing still for long periods. When you do have to stand still, keep your weight evenly distributed on both legs. Try standing with one foot a little forward of the other, changing the forward foot every few minutes to help reduce stiffness in your legs and lower back.

- High-heeled shoes require the body to make postural changes similar to those in the later stages of pregnancy *(see pages 156–159)*, placing considerable strain on the spine. So high heels should only be worn occasionally, and preferably not when you have to do a lot of standing or walking. Ideally, shoes should be flat or with a small, broad-based heel.

below *One of the most important steps that you can take towards ensuring a healthy back is to go for a brisk walk every day.*

- Remember that a healthy back requires plenty of exercise, so try to take a brisk walk every day, concentrating on your posture. When walking and running, the impact of the heel against the ground transmits a considerable shock force through the joints of the leg into the lower back. This can aggravate ankle, knee, hip and back problems. It is worth buying shoes with shock-absorbing properties in their heels, available from sports shops and in some everyday shoes. There are also shock-absorbing insoles slim enough to fit into most shoes.

- Lifting heavy and awkward items is a common cause of back problems. If you have to lift something heavy, try and get someone to help. When lifting on your own, stand squarely and as close to the object as possible, with your feet slightly apart. Keeping your back straight and your abdominal muscles tensed, squat down with the object in front of you. Holding it securely with both hands, keep your back as straight as possible and lift in one easy movement, with all the force coming from the muscles of your legs. Never twist your back, as this can cause a severe back strain. Always mentally prepare yourself for lifting, as injury can occur if you lift an item that is heavier than anticipated.

EXERCISES FOR THE WORKING DAY

CAR JOURNEYS

Driving for long periods of time places considerable strain on our backs, particularly for anyone who is either experiencing an episode of back pain or has recently recovered from one. Ideally, if you are still experiencing significant discomfort in your back it is advisable to avoid driving completely. If your journey really is necessary, ask someone else to drive you.

If driving is unavoidable it is wise to take some analgesics *(see page 53)* before you travel and make sure that you have some with you to take at the recommended time interval between doses. Also be sure to check on the packet that the medication will not make you drowsy if you are driving. Try to keep your journey time to an absolute minimum, but if you have to go on a long journey it is essential that you take frequent breaks so that you can change position, stretch and loosen your back muscles.

left *Failing to adjust your car seat correctly often results in back pain.*

right *Stowing your luggage in the boot of your car will help avoid the need for awkward twisting movements to the rear seat.*

The driving position

While the design of some car seats is better than others, the following steps will help to ensure the best position to reduce the strain on your back when driving:

1 Adjust your seat back so that you are sitting in an upright position, with minimal tension in your neck and shoulders.

below *The rising number of cars on our roads inevitably leads to longer journey times, frustration and increased tension, all of which puts greater stress on the muscles of our back, neck and shoulders.*

2 Sit well back into the seat so that both your pelvis and the small of your back are fully supported. Tilt your pelvis correctly *(see page 66)*.

3 Adjust the lumbar support (if your car is fitted with one) to maintain your lumbar curve, or use a small pad or rolled towel if there is insufficient support in the seat.

4 If possible, adjust the tilt of the squab of the seat so that it is as level as it can be. Alternatively, a thin wedge-shaped cushion can be used to achieve this effect.

5 Adjust the height of the seat and the reach and angle of the steering wheel so that your arms are in a comfortable outstretched position, with your elbows slightly bent. Ensure that you can reach the foot pedals comfortably, without any strain on your back.

6 Adjust your head restraint so that the middle of the restraint is level with the top of your ears. You risk severe injury to your cervical spine if your head restraint is too low because, in a collision, your head will be thrown backwards over the top of the restraint.

7 If you are changing your car, look for a model with plenty of seat and steering-wheel adjustments. If you have a chronic low-back problem, power-assisted steering and automatic transmission will help.

EXERCISES FOR THE WORKING DAY

EXERCISE WHILE TRAVELLING

It is quite possible to do some back exercises (such as the sitting pelvic tilt, *see page 68*) while you are sitting in your stationary car, or when you stop for a break. The change in posture and the stimulation of your circulation will do much to alleviate back problems. Some of the exercises recommended on these pages are also useful when you are travelling by aeroplane.

top right *When you have a long journey to make, remember to take frequent breaks, perhaps stopping for a picnic or a brief walk.*

In stressful driving conditions our usual reaction is to thrust our head (particularly the lower jaw) forward, clench our teeth and grip the steering wheel too firmly. All these reactions create tension, particularly in the neck and shoulders, but also in the back.

To help alleviate these symptoms of stress keep reminding yourself of the need to relax, purposefully dropping your shoulders away from your ears and lengthening your neck. One extremely useful technique is to open your mouth very wide, stretching your jaw muscles and releasing the tension (it may look odd to other drivers, though!). When we are in stressful situations we also tend to breathe too quickly and shallowly, so take a few slow, deep breaths every now and then.

Whether you are the driver or a passenger, try to change your sitting position regularly. Adults have the tendency to get into a car

and sit still. When they reach their destination they often feel very stiff. Children, however, fidget constantly and are invariably still full of energy at the end of the journey. Changing position helps to stimulate the circulation and uses different muscle groups, so try to move as much as you can and you should feel less stiff and a lot fresher at your journey's end.

Adjusting the angle of the back of the seat by a few degrees every half an hour is a very good way of relieving some of the tension in the lower back muscles. To help reduce tension in your neck, stretch your neck muscles gently, first by moving your right ear down towards your right shoulder and then your left ear down towards your left shoulder. If you are a passenger, flex your feet up and then point them down, as well as rolling them from side to side, in order to stimulate the circulation in your legs. This is particularly important when you are on a long flight.

Many of the office exercises can be adapted for those who drive for long periods. For safety, the journey should be broken every two hours so that you remain alert. Taking regular breaks also provides an ideal opportunity to do a few exercises.

Getting out of the car after a long journey can be quite a challenge if you have a painful back, as your muscles will have stiffened after sitting for too long. Therefore take a moment to plan the most comfortable way of getting out of the car. Choose a parking place where you can open the car door fully, unrestricted by other parked cars, kerbs, etc. You do not need to hunt for the parking space closest to your destination, as a short walk will be of benefit to you.

Open your car door fully and then swing both your legs around so that both feet are placed on the ground and you are sitting sideways on the car seat. From this position you can stand up without twisting your back and are much less likely

to experience pain. When you get back into your car simply reverse this action; lower yourself onto the car seat, then swing your legs round into the driving position. If your back is acutely painful and the journey is unavoidable, try sitting on a plastic bag as this will allow you to swivel round more easily.

Sitting sideways on the edge of your seat provides the ideal opportunity to do a seated flexion exercise *(see pages 69–71)* to gently stretch your back muscles prior to standing up. Now walk around for a few minutes, taking a few slow, deep breaths. Then do some of the standing stretches *(see pages 100–103)*, paying attention to your lower back, and some chest and shoulder stretches to relieve the tension in your upper body. If your legs are feeling stiff, do a standing quad and hamstring stretch *(see pages 106–109)* and then rise up onto your toes and down again several times to improve the circulation in your legs.

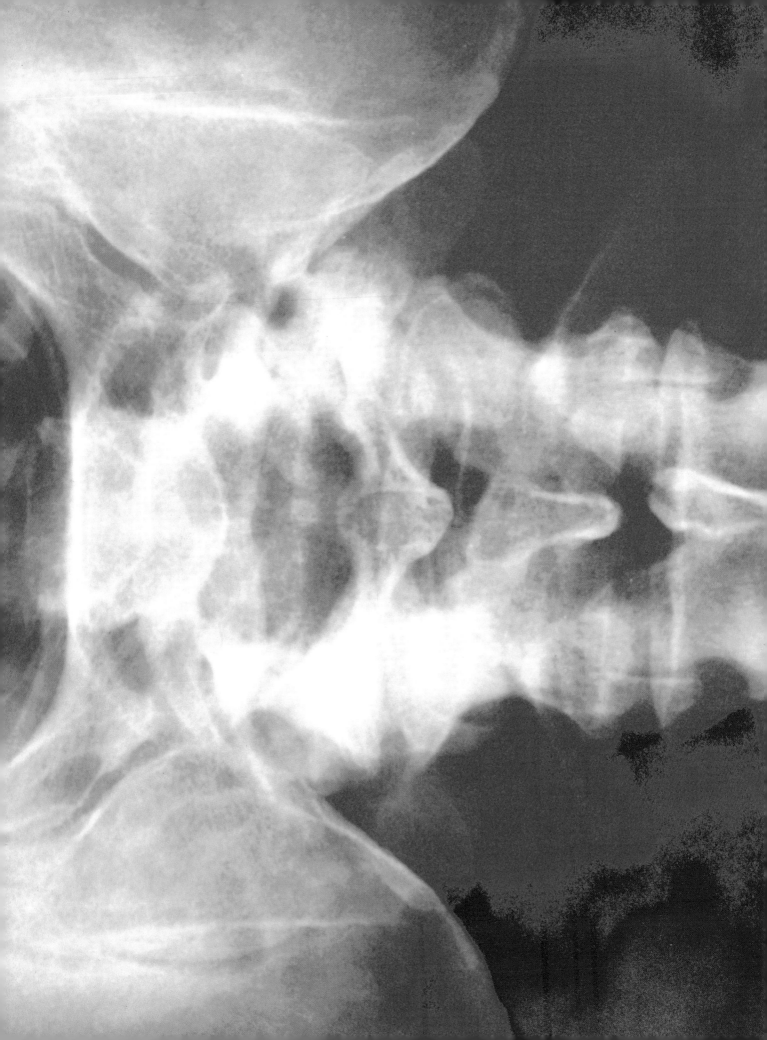

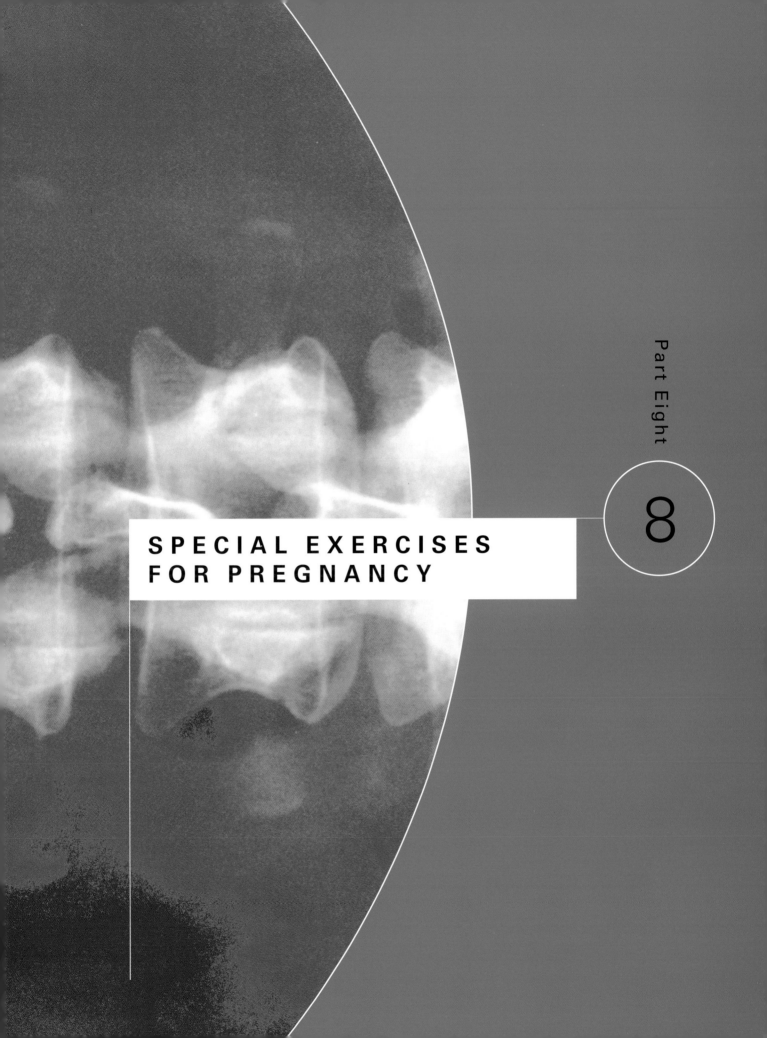

SPECIAL EXERCISES FOR PREGNANCY

INTRODUCTION

BACK PROBLEMS IN PREGNANCY

Low back pain is a common complaint in the later stages of pregnancy. As the pregnancy progresses, the rapidly enlarging abdomen requires significant postural changes to be made, and these are discussed in more detail on the following pages. These changes can give rise to discomfort and sometimes pain in the lower back. The best way to avoid back pain in pregnancy is to follow the advice in this section and, as well as doing the exercises on pages 160–161, take regular, gentle exercise such as walking. Always try to avoid placing unnecessary strain on your back, so avoid wearing high-heeled shoes, take extra care when lifting and avoid standing in one position for too long.

above *Hold your baby in front of you, rather than propped on one hip, to help avoid back strain.*

In the later stages of pregnancy hormonal changes help prepare the body for the impending birth, but these can also be a cause of backache. One of these hormones is relaxin, which, as the name suggests, has a relaxing effect, acting on the ligaments to allow for expansion of the birth canal in the pelvis during birth. Relaxin also relaxes the ligaments of other joints, including the spine, thus increasing the risk of low back strain.

During the latter part of pregnancy, some women can also experience an intense, sharp pain in the sacroiliac region *(see page 19)*, which may radiate into the groin. This pain is usually associated with twisting movements and is due to the effect of relaxin on the sacroiliac ligaments, which allows increased

mobility in the sacroiliac joints. To prevent this, avoid twisting and be careful when you are turning over in bed in order to reduce the risk of straining the sacroiliac joints. The problem usually resolves itself after pregnancy when hormone levels return to normal.

By paying particular attention to maintaining good posture *(see pages 148–149)*, by undertaking regular gentle exercise and by being extremely careful when bending and lifting while pregnant, the likelihood of suffering from backache can be reduced. Remember that your back is much more susceptible to strain while you are pregnant, so try and keep lifting to a minimum.

If you do have to lift heavy objects, then it is even more important than usual that you face

left *If you have just one item to carry, then clasp it to you.*

far left *Divide heavy loads into two equal parts to lessen the strain they impose on the back.*

the object that you are to pick up, rather than twisting in order to reach it. Keep your back straight and your abdominal muscles tensed, bending at the knees and making the lift come from your legs rather than from your back. Always try to avoid carrying heavy items, but if you do need to carry heavy or awkward loads, such as shopping, then divide the weight equally, carrying a similar weight in each hand. This will prevent your back being pulled to one side. If you are carrying just one bag, keep it hugged to your front, again so that you are not being pulled to one side.

After the birth

The likelihood of experiencing back problems after you have had the baby can be reduced by avoiding excessive weight gain during pregnancy, as you will therefore return to your pre-pregnancy weight soon after the birth.

Regaining your abdominal muscle tone by doing regular abdominal exercises will also help to minimize the stresses on your spine. Make sure that you follow the postural advice on page 99 so that your body regains its pre-pregnancy stance as soon as possible after the birth.

INTRODUCTION

POSTURE DURING PREGNANCY

The typical posture of a woman in later pregnancy is illustrated in the left-hand photograph opposite. Note how the enlarged abdomen appears to be pulling her forwards and downwards, stretching the abdominal muscles. This causes the pelvis to tip forward, exaggerating the lumbar curve, which in turn places additional strain on the thoracic and cervical spine. As the centre of gravity moves forward, the knees extend, the shoulders become more rounded and the head thrusts forward. As the normal postural curves are lost, the ligaments and muscles supporting the spine are put under considerable strain.

above *Carrying a child on one hip puts all the weight on one side and is a common cause of back strain.*

During the last few months of pregnancy it is most important to check and correct your posture constantly.

The key to improving your posture lies with your pelvis. If you tilt this correctly, maintaining the correct tone in your abdominal muscles, you will reduce the strain on the lumbar spine.

Try to imagine that your pelvis is a bowl that is full, almost to the brim, with liquid. When you stand with your pelvis tipped forward, the liquid runs over the top, but when you tilt your pelvis correctly the liquid is held within the bowl. Now, whenever you sit, stand or walk, remember to visualize your pelvis as a bowl full of liquid. Concentrate on keeping the liquid within the bowl and you will be more likely to hold your pelvis correctly and

consequently much less likely to suffer from backache. An added advantage is that you will maintain better tone in your abdominal muscles and therefore may regain your figure more quickly after the birth.

Standing while pregnant

When you are standing for any length of time, keep changing your position regularly. Try alternately placing one foot a little in front of the other and then changing, keeping your weight evenly distributed between both legs and ensuring that your knee joints are slightly flexed.

It is very important to avoid standing with most of your weight on one leg. In this position the joints of your weight-bearing leg are

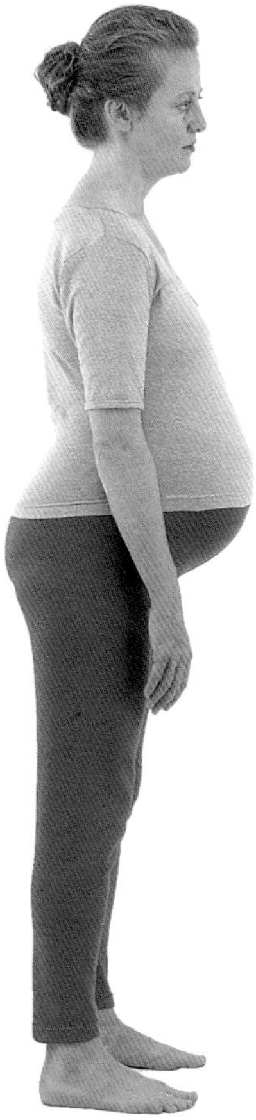

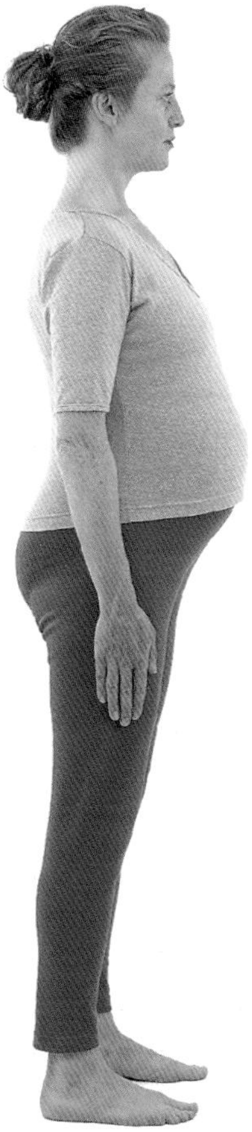

left *Remember to tilt your pelvis correctly and tense your abdominal muscles to protect your back while you are pregnant.*

far left *Poor posture during the latter months of pregnancy, with the pelvis tilted incorrectly, causes extra strain on the lower back.*

locked and your pelvis tilts to one side, causing considerable strain on your lumbar spine. This is a very common way for a mother to stand after the birth, with the baby supported on the weight-bearing hip. Instead, try holding the baby close to and in front of you, rather than at the side, and preferably supported by a sling.

Sitting while pregnant

As your pregnancy progresses you may find that sitting for long periods becomes increasingly uncomfortable. It is helpful therefore to keep changing your position, walking around frequently – at least every half an hour or so.

It will also become increasingly difficult to stand up from a low, deep chair, causing unnecessary strain in your back and sacroiliac joints *(see page 19)*. Therefore try to choose an upright and firm chair to sit it, and you can support your lumbar spine with a small cushion, if required.

Sit with both feet on the ground or with your feet raised on a foot stool. Never sit with your legs crossed at the knees, as this twists your pelvis and lumbar spine, as well as impairing the circulation in your legs.

Remember to tilt your pelvis correctly, sitting up tall and straight while keeping your shoulders relaxed. Sitting correctly will help to create as much space as possible for your baby, as well as helping to relieve congestion in your pelvis and legs and reducing the strain on your spine.

above *Remember to tighten your abdominal muscles when lifting, and to keep the child close to your body.*

EXERCISES FOR PREGNANCY

Much of the backache that occurs in later pregnancy, caused by the increasing weight of the growing foetus, can be alleviated by maintaining a correct posture. However, if you do experience backache, then the gentle exercises on these pages will help to stretch the muscles of the back and will provide you with additional relief.

SEATED PELVIC ROCK

You may find that a seated pelvic rock will help to relieve any aching in your back that you are experiencing. Do this as often as you wish, as it only takes a few minutes and is useful if you continue to work in a sedentary occupation.

1 **Starting position**
Sit on an upright chair or stool with your pelvis tilted correctly and both feet planted firmly on the floor.

Pelvic rock **2**
Allow your pelvis to rock forward a little (do not force it forward, however). Now tense your abdominal muscles and at the same time rock your pelvis back. At this point you should feel a pleasant gentle stretch throughout your lower back. Repeat this rhythmical rocking sequence a few times.

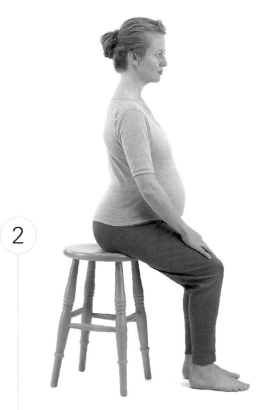

LYING PELVIC TILT

By performing an exaggerated pelvic tilt while you are lying down you will help to stretch the lower back muscles.

Lower back to floor

1

Lie on your back on a comfortable surface with your head resting on a cushion if you wish. Bend your legs, feet flat on the floor and knees hip-width apart. Now tense your abdominal muscles and tilt your pelvis so that your lower back is pressed to the floor. Hold this position for a slow count of ten, breathing normally throughout.

Lower back arched

2

Now tilt your pelvis the other way. Your back may arch slightly away from the floor, but do not force the movement. Return to the starting position. Repeat the sequence five times, and repeat the pelvic-tilt exercise several times during the day. While you are lying down take the chance to relax (see pages 74–75).

Pelvic-floor exercise

It is particularly important to strengthen the muscles of your pelvic floor after the birth of your baby. You will be taught this exercise by your midwife.

Pelvic-floor muscles support the contents of the pelvis (for example, the uterus, vagina, rectum and bladder). Weak muscles cannot do this effectively, possibly giving rise to complications such as stress incontinence (involuntary urination – for instance, when sneezing or coughing).

To perform the pelvic-floor exercise, slowly and gently contract the muscles around your vagina, drawing them inwards and upwards.

Initially you may find that you also tighten your rectal and abdominal muscles, but with a bit of practice you should be able to isolate the correct muscles. One way of learning how to do this is to tighten the muscles while urinating, stopping the flow for a count of five, relaxing and then tightening again.

When you are confident that you know how to tighten your pelvic-floor muscles correctly, the exercise can be done at any time, especially when you are sitting down. Try to make the contraction and relaxation very slow and smooth, timing them with your breathing. As you breathe in, slowly tighten your muscles; as you breathe out, relax them.

WATCHPOINT

● Do not force any of the movements in these exercises, and if you feel any sharp pain, stop immediately.

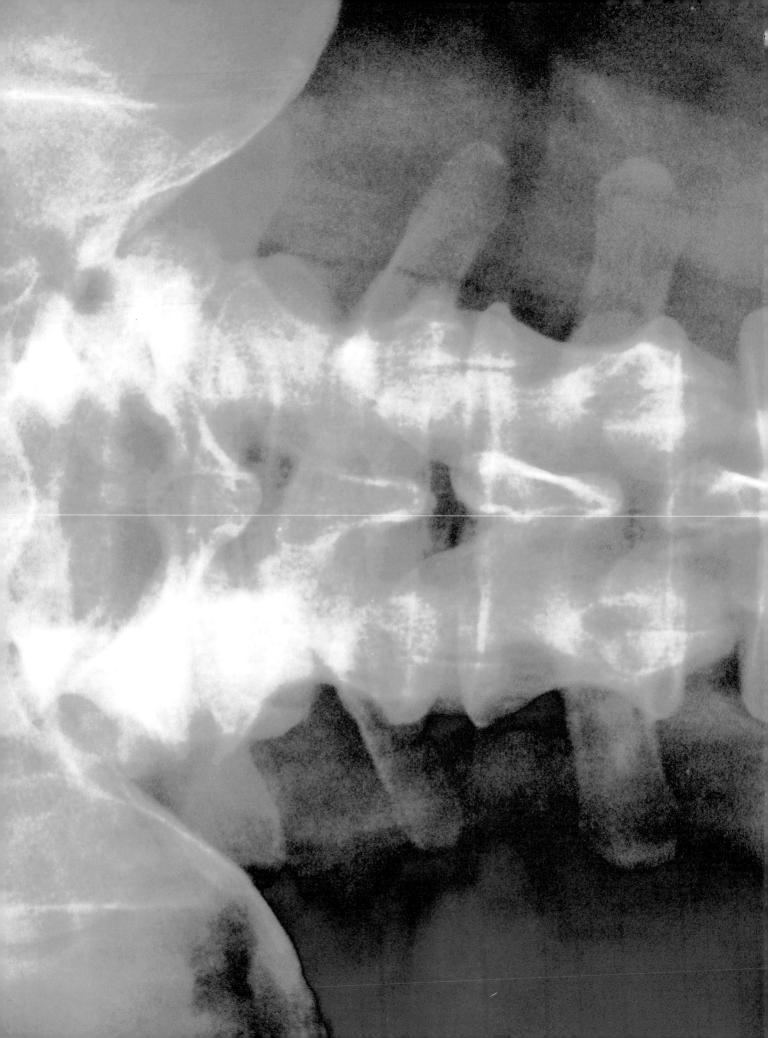

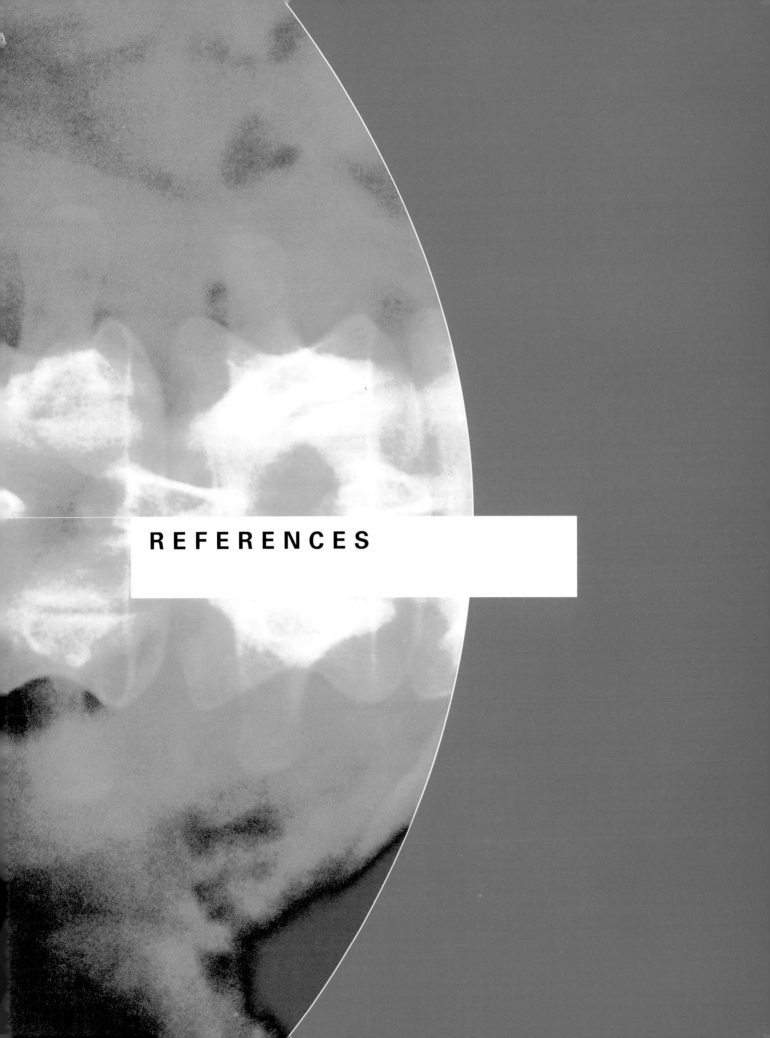

REFERENCES

GLOSSARY

A

Abdominal Relating to the part of the body lying between the chest and the pelvis.

Acute A condition that comes on suddenly and tends to be severe and of brief duration.

Analgesic A medication that relieves pain.

Annulus fibrosus The fibrous outer covering of an intervertebral disc; it encloses the jelly-like nucleus pulposus.

Anti-inflammatory A substance that relieves inflammation.

Atlas The top bone of the cervical spine, which supports the skull.

C

Cardiovascular Relating to the heart and the system of blood vessels that carry blood throughout the body.

Cartilage A robust, flexible connective tissue that covers the surfaces of joints.

Cervical vertebrae The seven bones of the neck.

Chiropractor A practitioner of a manipulative therapy.

Chronic A long-standing condition that shows little or no improvement.

Coccyx The tailbone at the base of the spine, attached to the sacrum.

Congenital A condition that exists from birth.

D

Degeneration A deterioration of tissue or joint to a less healthy state.

Disc *See* Intervertebral disc.

E

Extension A backward-bending movement of the spine or straightening of a limb.

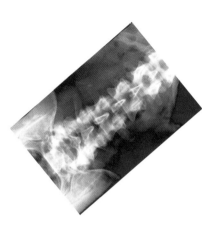

F

Facet joint A joint that guides movement of the vertebrae and gives stability to the spine; facet joints are found in pairs between vertebrae.

Flexion A forward-bending movement of the spine or bending of a limb.

Fracture A break in a bone.

I

Intervertebral disc A strong, flexible cushion that lies between the vertebrae, absorbing shocks and permitting movement of the spine.

Intervertebral foramen (pl. foramina) A small hole or channel on each side of a vertebra, through which the spinal nerves pass.

J

Joint The place where two or more bones meet and allow movement to occur.

K

Kyphosis An exaggerated forward bending of the spine.

L

Lateral flexion A side-bending movement of the spine.

Ligament A band of tough, fibrous tissue that connects two bones at a joint (or supports an organ of the body); ligaments bind the vertebrae together and help make the spine stable but flexible.

Lumbar vertebrae The five bones of the lower back.

M

Motor nerve A nerve that carries impulses from the brain via the spinal cord in the muscles.

Muscle A bundle of fibres that produce movement when they contract and relax.

Muscle spasm Tension caused by the muscles contracting more tightly than normal.

N

Nerve receptor A sensor that registers different types of sensation in the body.

NSAID Non-steroidal anti-inflammatory drug.

Nucleus pulposus The jelly-like substance inside each intervertebral disc; it is contained by the annulus fibrosus.

O

Osteoarthritis A degenerative disease of the joints, most commonly affecting those that are weight-bearing.

Osteopath A practitioner of a health-care profession that lays its main emphasis on the diagnosis and treatment of musculoskeletal disorders.

Osteoporosis A loss of density in the bones, leaving them more prone to fracture; it is more prevalent in women than it is in men.

P

Pelvis A basin-shaped bony structure at the lower end of the trunk, consisting of two innominate bones and the sacrum.

Physiotherapist A practitioner who treats injury by physical methods, including manipulation, massage, remedial exercise and heat treatment.

Prolapsed intervertebral disc The medical term for a slipped disc.

R

Referred pain Pain that manifests in a different part of the body from the site of the actual problem.

Relaxin A hormone produced in pregnant women that relaxes the ligaments, allowing for expansion of the birth canal in preparation for childbirth.

Rotation A turning movement of the spine.

S

Sacroiliac joint One of two joints that lie between the sacrum and the ilium at the back of the pelvis.

Sacrum A triangular bone forming part of the pelvis; it consists of five fused vertebrae.

Scoliosis A side-bending deformity of the spine.

Sensory nerve A nerve that carries sensations of pain from the skin and other sensory organs to the spinal cord.

Slipped disc A term sometimes used to describe a disc that bulges or herniates, pressing on ligaments, nerves or the spinal cord; properly known as a prolapsed intervertebral disc.

'Soft' joint A joint that is held in a slightly flexed position that prepares it for movement.

Spinal cord A cylinder of nervous tissue that runs down the spinal cord from the brain to the upper lumbar region and transmits messages to and from the brain.

Spinal nerve One of 31 pairs of nerves connected to the spinal cord; each group serves a separate area of the body and carries both motor and sensory fibres.

Sprain An injury to a joint, resulting in damage to the ligaments that surround it.

T

Thoracic vertebrae The 12 bones of the upper and middle back.

V

Vertebra One of the bones that make up the spine; there are seven cervical vertebrae, 12 thoracic vertebrae and five lumbar vertebrae.

Visualization The creation of visual pictures in the mind to achieve relaxation.

W

Whiplash injury An injury to the neck, often caused by a car accident.

REFERENCES

USEFUL ADDRESSES

When you experience a debilitating back problem it is often confusing to know where to go for advice. For many people their general practitioner is the first port of call. Family doctors will often prescribe pain-relieving medication and sometimes muscle-relaxant drugs if the back pain is severe. If the problem is the result of a significant physical trauma, or your doctor suspects the back pain might be referred from another area of the body or be due to another cause, you may be referred for X-rays, scans or other investigations. You may also wish to seek the specialist opinion of an osteopath, chiropractor or physiotherapist. These are practitioners who have received specialist training in the diagnosis and manual treatment of back problems. You can consult them privately without a referral from your doctor. In the UK all osteopaths must be registered with the General Osteopathic Council, chiropractors with the General Chiropractic Council and physiotherapists with the Chartered Society of Physiotherapy. These bodies will be able to provide you with details of your nearest practitioner.

Arthritis Care
18 Stephenson Way
London NW1 2HD, UK
Tel: 020 7380 6500
Fax: 020 7380 6505
Helpline: 080 8800 4050/020 7380 6555

Arthritis Foundation of Ireland
1 Clanwilliam Square
Grand Canal Quay, Dublin 2, Ireland
Tel: 01 661 8188

Arthritis Foundation of New Zealand (Inc.)
Ninth Floor, 169 The Terrace
Wellington, PO Box 10-020
New Zealand
Tel: 04 472 1427
Fax: 04 472 7066

**BackCare: The National
Organization for Healthy Backs**
16 Elmtree Road, Teddington
Middlesex TW11 BST, UK
Tel: 020 8977 5474
Fax: 020 8943 5318

British Acupuncture Council
63 Jedd Road, London W12 9HQ, UK
Tel: 020 8753 0399
Email: info@acupuncture.org.uk

British Medical Acupuncture Society
12 Marbury House, Higher Whitley
Warrington, Cheshire WA4 4QW, UK
Tel: 01925 730727
Fax: 01925 730492
Email: Admin@medical-
acupuncture.org.uk

Chartered Society of Physiotherapy
14 Bedford Row
London WC1R 4ED, UK
Tel: 020 7306 6663/4/5
Fax: 020 7306 6611

Chiropractic Association of Ireland
19 Robinstown, Mullingar
County Westmeath
Ireland
Tel: 044 483 74
Fax: 044 401 65

169

Chiropractors' Association of Australia Ltd
Suite 4, 148 Station Street
Penrith NSW 2750, Australia
Tel: 02 4731 8011

Council for Massage Therapy Organizations
46 Millmead Way, Maltings Walk
Hertford, Hertfordshire, UK

Foundation for Integrated Medicine
International House, 59 Compton Road
London N1 2YT, UK
Tel: 020 7688 1881

General Chiropractic Council
344–54 Gray's Inn Road
London WC1X 8BP, UK
Tel: 020 7713 5155
Fax: 020 7713 5844
Email: enquiries@gcc-uk.org

General Osteopathic Council
Osteopathy House, 176 Tower Bridge Road
London SE1 3LU, UK
Tel: 020 7357 6655
Fax: 020 7357 0011

Irish Society of Chartered Physiotherapists
Royal College of Surgeons
123 St Stephen's Green
Dublin 2, Ireland
Tel: 01 402 2100
Fax: 01 402 2160
Email: info@iscp.ie

National Osteoporosis Society
PO Box 10, Radstock
Bath BA3 3YB, UK
Tel: 01761 471771
Helpline: 01761 472721
Fax: 01761 471104
Email: info@nos.org.uk

New Zealand Society of Physiotherapists
Level 6, Wang House, 201 Willis Street
PO Box 27 386, Wellington
New Zealand
Tel: 4 801 6500
Fax: 4 801 5571

Society of Teachers of the Alexander Technique
20 London House, 266 Fulham Road
London SW10 9EL, UK
Tel: 020 7351 0828
Email: enquiries@stat.org.uk

Yoga Biomedical Trust
Yoga Therapy Centre
Royal Homeopathic Hospital
60 Great Ormond Street
London WC1N 3HR, UK
Tel: 020 7419 7195

WEBSITES

Arthritis Care:
http://www.arthritiscare.org.uk

Arthritis Foundation of Ireland:
http://www.arthritis-foundation.com

Arthritis Foundation of New Zealand (Inc.):
http://www.arthritis.org.nz

Arthritis Research Association:
http://www.arc.org.uk

Australian Osteopathic Association:
http://www.osteopathic.com.au

Australian Physiotherapy Association:
http://www. physiotherapy.asn.au

BackCare: The National Organization for Healthy Backs:
http://www.backpain.org

Back Pain: Patient UK:
http://www.patient.co.uk

British Acupuncture Council:
http://www.acupuncture.org.uk

British Chiropractic Association:
http://www.chiropractic-uk.co.uk

British Medical Acupuncture Association:
http://www.medical-acupuncture.co.uk

British Orthopaedic Association:
http://www.boa.ac.uk

Chartered Society of Physiotherapy:
http://www.csphysio.org.uk

Chiropractic Association of Ireland:
http://www.chiropractic.ie

Chiropractic Association of South Africa:
http://www.chiropractic.co.za

Chiropractors' Association of Australia (National) Ltd:
http://www.caa.com.au

Facts about pain at the back of the head:
http://www.netdoctor.co.uk/diseases/facts/neckpains.htm

Foundation of Integrated Medicine:
http://www.www.fimed.org

General Chiropractic Council:
http://www.gcc-uk.org

General Osteopathic Council:
http://www.osteopathy.org.uk

Information about back pain:
http://www.backpainreliefonline.com/

Irish Society of Chartered Physiotherapists:
http://www.iscp.ie

National Center for Complementary and Alternative Medicine: information:
http://www.nccam.nih.gov/nccam

National Osteoporosis Society:
http://www.nos.org.uk

Neck pain information:
http://www.spineuniverse.com

New Zealand Society of Physiotherapists:
http://www.nzsp.org.nz

NINDS back pain information:
http://www.ninds.nih.gov/help.htm

Society of Teachers of the Alexander Technique:
http://www.stat.org.uk

South African Natural Health Network:
http://www.naturalhealth.co.za

Yoga Biomedical Trust:
http://www.yogatherapy.org

Deborah Fielding
teaches back-care exercises to individuals, small groups and back-pain self-help organizations. For further information contact her at: Email: healthyback@blueyonder.co.uk or visit her website: http://www.healthyback.pwp.blueyonder.co.uk

REFERENCES AND FURTHER READING

ANDERSON, BOB, *Stretching,* Pelham Books, 1985

ANON, *Understanding Back Trouble,* A Consumer Publication, Which? Books, 1991

ASPDEN, R. M., AND PORTER, R. W., *Lumbar Spine Disorders: Current Concepts,* World Scientific Publishing, 1995

BARTLEY, R. ET AL., *Management of Low Back Pain in Primary Care,* Butterworth-Heinemann, 2001

Basic Back Care, National Organization for Healthy Backs, 1999

BRITISH MEDICAL ASSOCIATION, *Complete Family Health Encyclopedia,* Dorling Kindersley, 1990

BROURMAN, SHERRY, AND RODMAN, RANDY, *Walk Yourself Well: Eliminate Back, Neck, Shoulder, Knee, Hip and Other Structural Pain Forever – Without Surgery or Drugs,* Hyperion Books, 1999

BROWNSTEIN, ART, *Healing Back Pain Naturally,* Newleaf, 2000

BURN, LOIC, *Back and Neck Pain: The Facts,* Oxford University Press, 1999

CAMPBELL, DR ANTHONY, *Good Health: Back – Your 100 Questions Answered,* Newleaf, 2001

CYRIAX, JAMES, *Textbook of Orthopaedic Medicine,* vol. 1, 8th edition, Ballière Tindall, 1984

DAVIES, I. J. T., *Postgraduate Medicine,* 5th edition, Chapman and Hall, 1991

FERGUSON, ANDREW, *Back and Neck Pain,* Pelham Books, 1988

FISHMAN, LOREN, AND ARDMAN, CAROL, *Back Pain: How to Relieve Low Back Pain and Sciatica,* W. W. Norton, 1999

GOLDMAN, DAVID R., AND HOROWITZ, DAVID A., *American College of Physicians' Home Medical Guide: Back Pain,* Dorling Kindersley, 2000

HAGE, MIKE, *The Back Pain Book: A Self-Help Guide for Daily Relief of Neck & Back Pain,* Peachtree Publishers, 1992

HOCHSCHULER, STEPHEN, *Back in Shape: A Back Owner's Manual,* Houghton Mifflin, 1991

HOWARD, NIGEL, *Alternative Answers to Back Problems: The Complete Conventional and Alternative Guide to Treating Back Pain,* Reader's Digest Association, 2001

MASLINE, SHELAGH, *Back Pain: What You Need to Know,* Time-Life Books, 1999

MASSENGALE, DEE, *The Guide to a Better Back: A Back Pain Sufferer's Handbook for Exercise and Daily Living,* S. Hunter Publishing, 1988

MELZACK, RONALD, AND WALL, PATRICK, *The Challenge of Pain* (revised edition), Penguin Books, 1996

MURTAGH, JOHN EDWARD, *Back Pain and Spinal Manipulation,* Butterworth-Heinemann, 1997

D'ORAZIO, BRIAN P., *Low Back Pain Handbook,* Butterworth-Heinemann, 1998

Osteoporosis: Causes, Prevention and Treatment, National Osteoporosis Society, 1999

PARKER, HELEN, AND MAIN, CHRIS J., *Living with Back Pain,* Manchester University Press, 1990

Reader's Digest Family Guide to Alternative Medicine, Reader's Digest, 1991

RICHARDSON, CAROLYN ET AL., *Therapeutic Exercise for Spinal Segmental Stabilisation in Lower Back Pain,* Churchill Livingstone, 1998

ROBINSON, LYNNE, AND THOMSON, GORDON, *Body Control the Pilates Way,* Pan Books, 1998

SALMANS, SANDRA, *Back Pain: Questions You Have...Answers You Need,* People's Medical Society, 1995

SARNO, JOHN E., *Healing Back Pain,* Time Warner International, 1991

SARNO, JOHN E., *Mind over Back Pain: A Radically New Approach to the Diagnosis and Treatment of Back Pain,* Berkeley Publishing, 1999

SCOTT, JUDITH, *Good-Bye to Bad Backs: Simple Stretching and Strengthening Exercises for Alignment and Freedom from Lower Back Pain,* Princeton Book Co., 1993

STODDARD, DR ALLEN, *The Back: Relief from Pain,* Martin Dunitz, 1979

SUTCLIFFE, DR JENNY, *Solving Back Problems,* Marshall Publishing, 1999

SWAYZEE, NANCY L., *Breathworks for Your Back: Strengthening Your Back from the Inside Out,* Avon Books, 1998

WADDELL, GORDON, *The Back Pain Revolution,* Churchill Livingstone, 1998

WARWICK, ROGER, AND WILLIAMS, PETER L., *Gray's Anatomy,* 35th edition, Longmans, 1973

REFERENCES

INDEX

REFERENCES **INDEX CONTINUED**

REFERENCES

PICTURE CREDITS